C000252611

Lectionary
Advent 2012 to the eve of Advent 2013 (Year C)

Church House Publishing

Published by	Church House Publishing
	Church House
	Great Smith Street
	London SW1P 3AZ

Compilation © *The Archbishops' Council 2012*

ISBN 978-0-7151-2201-3 (standard)
978-0-7151-2202-0 (large)

Authorization The Common Worship Calendar and Lectionaries are authorized pursuant to Canon B 2 of the Canons of the Church of England for use until further resolution of the General Synod of the Church of England.

Copyright and Acknowledgements *The Revised Common Lectionary* is copyright © The Consultation on Common Texts: 1992. The Church of England adaptations to the Principal Service Lectionary are copyright © The Archbishops' Council, as are the Second and Third Service Lectionaries and the Weekday Lectionary for Morning and Evening Prayer.

The Daily Eucharistic Lectionary derives, with some adaptation, from the *Ordo Lectionum Missae* of the Roman Catholic Church and is reproduced by permission of The International Commission on English in the Liturgy.

Edited by Jonathan Goodall
Designed by Derek Birdsall & John Morgan/Omnific
Typeset by RefineCatch Ltd, Bungay, Suffolk
Printed in England by Core Publications

Contents of this booklet

This booklet gives details of the full range of possibilities envisaged in the liturgical calendar and lectionary of Common Worship. Its use as a tool for the preparation of worship will require the making of several choices based first on the general celebration of the Christian year by the Church of England as a whole; second on the customary pattern of calendar in the diocese, parish and place of worship; and third on the pattern of services locally.

The **first column** comprises the Calendar of the Church with the days of the year. Observances that are mandatory are printed either in **bold** type (Sundays), in **bold** type (Principal Feasts and Holy Days) or in roman (Festivals). Optional celebrations (Lesser Festivals) and Commemorations are printed in ordinary roman type and *italic* type respectively.

The **second column** comprises (a) the readings and psalms for the Principal Service on Sundays, Principal Feasts and Holy Days, and Festivals, and (b) Holy Communion readings and psalms for other days of the week. On the Sundays after Trinity, the Old Testament reading and its psalm are divided into two smaller columns, indicating a choice between a 'continuous' reading week by week or a reading 'related' to the Gospel for that day.

The **third column** comprises (a) the Third Service readings and psalms for Sundays, Principal Feasts and Holy Days, and Festivals, and (b) the readings and psalms for weekday Morning Prayer.

The **fourth column** comprises (a) the Second Service readings and psalms for Sundays, Principal Feasts and Holy Days, and Festivals, and (b) the readings and psalms for weekday Evening Prayer.

An **Additional Weekday Lectionary**, intended particularly for use in places of worship that attract occasional rather than daily worshippers, is provided on pages 67–75. It can be used either at Morning or Evening Prayer.

Common of the Saints

General readings and psalms for saints' days can be found on pages 78–82; for some particular celebrations, other readings are suggested there.

Special Occasions

Readings and psalms for special occasions can be found on pages 78–84.

Liturgical colours

Appropriate liturgical colours are suggested in this booklet. They are not mandatory; traditional or local use may be followed.

Colours are indicated by single letters: the first (always upper case) for the season or Festival; and occasionally a second (lower case) for an optional celebration on that day. Thus, for example, *Gr* for the celebration of a Lesser Festival whose liturgical colour is red, in an otherwise 'green' season. The following abbreviations are used:

The following abbreviations are used:

G	Green
P or p	Purple or Violet
P(La)	Purple or Lent array
R or r	Red
W or w	White (Gold is indicated where its use would be appropriate)

Notes on the Lectionary

Sundays, Principal Feasts and Holy Days and Festivals

Three sets of psalms and readings are provided for each Sunday, Principal Feast or Holy Day and Festival.

The **Principal Service lectionary** (based on the Revised Common Lectionary) is intended for use at the principal service of the day (whether this service is Holy Communion or some other authorized form). In most Church communities, this is likely to be the mid-morning service, but the minister is free to decide which service time normally constitutes the Principal Service of the day. This lectionary may be used twice if required – for example, at an early celebration of Holy Communion and then again at a later one.

If only **two readings** are used at the Principal Service and that service is Holy Communion, the second reading must always be the Gospel reading. When the Principal Service lectionary is used at a service other than Holy Communion, the Gospel reading need not always be chosen.

The **Second Service lectionary** is intended for a second main service. In many churches, this lectionary may be the appropriate provision for a Sunday afternoon or evening service. A Gospel reading is always provided so that this lectionary can, if necessary, be used where the second main service is a celebration of Holy Communion.

The **Third Service lectionary**, with shorter readings, is intended where a third set of psalms and readings is needed and is most appropriate for use at an office. A Gospel reading is not always provided, so this lectionary is not suitable for use at Holy Communion.

Weekdays

The Common Worship Weekday Lectionary authorized by the General Synod in 2005 comprises a lectionary (with psalms) for Holy Communion, a lectionary for Morning and Evening Prayer, and tables of psalms for Morning and Evening Prayer.

The **Daily Eucharistic Lectionary** (based on the Roman Catholic daily eucharistic lectionary) is a semi-continuous two-year lectionary with a wide use of scripture, though not complete coverage of the Bible. Two readings are provided for each day, the first from either the Old or New Testament, the second always a Gospel. Psalm provision is intended to be a brief response to the first reading. It is for use at Holy Communion normally in places with a daily or near-daily celebration with a regular congregation. It may also be used as an office lectionary.

The **lectionary for Morning and Evening Prayer** always provides two readings for each office, the first from the Old Testament and the second from the New Testament. These are generally in sequence. One of the New Testament readings for any particular day is from the Gospels.

The **psalms for Morning and Evening Prayer** follow a sequential pattern in Ordinary Time (apart from the period from All Saints to the beginning of Advent).

In the periods from All Saints until 18 December, from the Epiphany until the Presentation of Christ in the Temple (Candlemas), from Ash Wednesday until Palm Sunday, and from the Monday after Easter Week until Pentecost, there is a choice of psalms at Morning and Evening Prayer. The psalms printed first reflect the theme of the season. Alternatively, the psalms from the Ordinary Time cycle may be used. The two sets are separated by 'or'.

From 19 December until the Epiphany and from the Monday of Holy Week until the Saturday of Easter Week, only seasonal psalms are provided.

Where more than one psalm is given, one psalm (printed in **bold**) may be used as the sole psalm at that office.

Guidance on how these options for saying the psalms are expressed typographically can be found in the 'Notes on the Lectionary' below.

A further cycle is provided (see table on page 85), which is largely the monthly sequential cycle of psalms given in the *Book of Common Prayer*.

A single psalm for use by those who only say one office each day is provided in Prayer During the Day in *Common Worship: Daily Prayer*.

An **Additional Weekday Lectionary**, intended particularly for use in places of worship that attract occasional rather than daily worshippers, is provided on pages 67–75. It can be used either at Morning or Evening Prayer. Psalmody is not provided and should be taken from provision outlined above.

Using the Lectionary tables

All **Bible references** (except to the Psalms) are to the *New Revised Standard Version* (New York, 1989). Those who use other Bible translations should check the verse numbers against the *NRSV*. Each reference gives book, chapter and verse, in that order.

References to the Psalms are to the Common Worship psalter, published in *Common Worship: Services and Prayers for the Church of England* (2000) and *Common Worship: Daily Prayer* (2005). A table showing the verse number differences between this and the psalter in the *Book of Common Prayer* is provided on the Common Worship web site (http://www.churchofengland.org/prayer-worship/worship/texts).

Options in the provision of readings or psalms are presented in the following ways:

¶ square brackets [xx] give either optional additional verses or Psalms, or a shorter alternative;

¶ 'or' indicates a simple choice between two alternative readings or courses of psalms;

¶ a psalm printed in **bold** may be used as the sole psalm at that office;

¶ on weekdays a psalm printed in parentheses (xx) is omitted if it has been used as the opening canticle at that office;

¶ a psalm marked with an asterisk may be shortened if desired.

Where a reading from the **Apocrypha** is offered, an alternative Old Testament reading is provided.

In the choice of **readings other than the Gospel** reading, the minister should ensure that, in any year, a balance is maintained between readings from the Old and New Testaments and that, where a particular biblical book is appointed to be read over several weeks, the choice ensures that the continuity of one book is not lost.

On the Sundays after Trinity, the Principal Service Lectionary provides **alternative Old Testament readings and psalms**. References in the left-hand column (under the heading 'Continuous') offer a *semi-continuous* reading of Old Testament texts. Such a reading and its complementary psalmody stand independently of the other readings. References in the right-hand column (under the heading 'Related') *relate* the Old Testament reading and the psalm to the Gospel reading. One column should be followed for the whole sequence of Sundays after Trinity.

The Lectionary 2012–2013

The Sunday and festal readings for 2 December 2012 (the First Sunday of Advent) to 30 November 2013 (St Andrew's Day, the eve of Advent Sunday) are from **Year C**, which offers a semi-continuous reading of Luke's Gospel at the Principal Service on Sundays throughout the year.

The weekday readings for Holy Communion are from **Year One** of the Daily Eucharistic Lectionary (DEL).

Office readings are from Table 2 of the Weekday Lectionary: at Morning Prayer, Old Testament 2a (seasonal time) and 2b (ordinary time), and New Testament 2; and, at Evening Prayer, Old Testament 1 and New Testament 1.

Notes on the Calendar 2 December 2012 — 30 November 2013

These notes are based on the Rules to Order the Christian Year (*Common Worship: Times and Seasons*, pages 24–30).

Sundays

All Sundays celebrate the paschal mystery of the death and resurrection of the Lord. They also reflect the character of the seasons in which they are set.

Principal Feasts

On these days (printed in **bold**) Holy Communion is celebrated in every cathedral and parish church, and this celebration, required by Canon B 14, may not be displaced by any other celebration, and may only be dispensed with in accordance with the provision of Canon B 14A.

Except in the case of Christmas Day and Easter Day, the celebration of the Feast *begins with Evening Prayer on the day before the Feast*, and the Collect at that Evening Prayer is that of the Feast. In the case of Christmas Eve and Easter Eve, there is proper liturgical provision (including a Collect) for the whole day.

The Presentation of Christ in the Temple (Candlemas) is celebrated on either Saturday 2 February or Sunday 3 February. **The Annunciation of Our Lord to the Blessed Virgin Mary** (25 March), falling on the Monday of Holy Week, is transferred to the Monday after the Second Sunday of Easter (8 April). **All Saints' Day** may be celebrated on Sunday 3 November (replacing the Fourth Sunday before Advent), with or without a supplementary celebration on Friday 1 November.

Other Principal Holy Days

These days (printed in **bold**), and the liturgical provision for them, may not be displaced by any other celebration.

Ash Wednesday (13 February) and **Maundy Thursday** (28 March) are Principal Holy Days. On both these days Holy Communion is celebrated in every cathedral or parish church, except where there is dispensation under Canon B 14A.

Good Friday (29 March) is a Principal Holy Day.

Eastertide

The paschal character of **the Great Fifty Days of Easter**, from Easter Day (31 March) to Pentecost (19 May), should be celebrated throughout the season, and should not be displaced by other celebrations. No Festival day may be celebrated in Easter Week; and nor may any Festival – except for a Patronal or Dedication Festival—displace the celebration of a Sunday (a memorial of the resurrection) during Eastertide. The paschal character of the season should be retained on those weekdays when saints' days are celebrated.

The three days before Ascension Day (6–8 May) are customarily observed as **Rogation Days**, when prayer is offered for God's blessing on the fruits of the earth and on human labour.

The nine days **after Ascension Day until the eve of Pentecost** (10–18 May) are observed as days of prayer and preparation for the celebration of the outpouring of the Holy Spirit.

Ordinary Time

Ordinary Time comprises two periods in the year: first, the period from the day after the Presentation of Christ in the Temple until the day before Ash Wednesday, and second, that from the day after Pentecost until the day before the First Sunday of Advent.

During Ordinary Time, there is no seasonal emphasis, except that the period between All Saints' Day and the First Sunday of Advent is a time to celebrate and reflect upon the reign of Christ in earth and heaven.

Festivals

These days (printed in roman), and the liturgical provision for them, are not usually displaced. For each day there is full liturgical provision for a Principal, Second and Third Service, and an optional so-called First Evening Prayer on the evening before the Festival where this is required.

Festivals may *not* be celebrated on Sundays in Advent, Lent or Eastertide, the Baptism of Christ, Ascension Day, Trinity Sunday or Christ the King, or weekdays between Palm Sunday and the Second Sunday of Easter.

Otherwise, Festivals falling on a Sunday—namely in 2013 Michael and All Angels (falling on the Eighteenth Sunday after Trinity)—may be kept on that Sunday or transferred to the Monday (or, at the discretion of the minister, to the next suitable weekday).

Certain Festivals (namely, Matthias the Apostle, the Visit of the BVM to Elizabeth, Thomas the Apostle, and the Blessed Virgin Mary) have customary alternative dates (see p.8). The Festival of the Blessed Virgin Mary may, in 2013, be celebrated on Sunday 8 September.

The Thursday after Trinity Sunday (30 May) may be observed as the **Day of Thanksgiving for the Institution of Holy Communion** (sometimes known as *Corpus Christi*), and may be kept as a Festival.

Other Celebrations

Mothering Sunday falls on the Fourth Sunday of Lent (10 March). Alternative prayers and readings are provided for the Principal Service. **Bible Sunday** may be celebrated on 27 October, replacing the Last Sunday after Trinity, and appropriate prayers and readings are provided.

Local Celebrations

The celebration of **the patron saint or the title of a church** is kept either as a Festival or as a Principal Feast.

The **Dedication Festival** of a church is the anniversary of the date of its dedication or consecration. This is kept either as a Festival or as a Principal Feast. When kept as Principal Feasts, the Patronal and Dedication Festivals may be transferred to the nearest Sunday, unless that day is already a Principal Feast or one of the following days: the First Sunday of Advent, the Baptism of Christ, the First Sunday of Lent, the Fifth Sunday of Lent, or Palm Sunday. If the actual date is not known, the Dedication Festival may be celebrated on 6 October (replacing the Nineteenth Sunday after Trinity), or on 27 October (replacing the Last Sunday after Trinity), or on a suitable date chosen locally. Readings can be found on page 77.

Harvest Thanksgiving may be celebrated on

any Sunday in autumn, replacing the provision for that day, provided it does not displace any Principal Feast or Festival.

Diocesan and other local provision may be made in **the calendar of the saints** to supplement the general calendar, in accordance with Canon B 6, paragraph 5.

Lesser Festivals

Lesser Festivals (printed in ordinary roman type, in black) are observed in a manner appropriate to a particular place. Each is provided with a Collect, which may supersede the Collect of the week. For certain Lesser Festivals a complete set of Eucharistic readings is provided, and for others appropriate readings may be selected from the Common of the Saints (see pages 78–84). These readings may, at the minister's discretion, supersede the Daily Eucharistic Lectionary (DEL). The weekday psalms and readings at Morning and Evening Prayer are not usually superseded by those for Lesser Festivals, but at the minister's discretion psalms and readings provided on these days for use at Holy Communion may be used instead at Morning or Evening Prayer.

The minister may be selective in the Lesser Festivals that are observed and may also keep some, or all of them, as Commemorations, perhaps especially in Advent, Lent and Easter where the character of the season ought to be sustained. If the Day of Thanksgiving for the Institution of Holy Communion (30 May) is not kept as a Festival, it may be kept as a Lesser Festival.

When a Lesser Festival falls on a Principal Feast or Holy Day, a Festival, a Sunday, or on a weekday between Palm Sunday and the Second Sunday of Easter, its celebration is normally omitted for that year. However, where there is sufficient reason, it may, at the discretion of the minister, be celebrated on the nearest available day.

Commemorations

Commemorations (printed in *italic*) are made by a mention in prayers of intercession. They are not provided with Collect, Psalm and Readings, and do not replace the usual weekday provision at Holy Communion or at Morning and Evening Prayer.

The minister may be selective in the Commemorations that are made:

Only where there is an established celebration in the wider Church or where the day has a special local significance may a Commemoration be observed as a Lesser Festival, with liturgical provision from the Common of the Saints (pages 78–84).

In designating a Commemoration as a Lesser Festival, the minister must remember the need to maintain the spirit of the season, especially of Advent, Lent and Easter.

Days of Discipline and Self-Denial

The weekdays of Lent and every Friday in the year are days of discipline and self-denial, with the exception of Principal Feasts, Festivals outside Lent, and Fridays from Easter Day to Pentecost. The day preceding a Principal Feast may also be appropriately kept as a day of discipline and self-denial in preparation for the Feast.

Ember Days

Ember Days should be kept, under the bishop's directions, in the week before an ordination as days of prayer for those to be ordained deacon or priest.

Ember Days may also be kept even when there is no ordination in the diocese as more general days of prayer for those who serve the Church in its various ministries, both ordained and lay, and for vocations. Traditionally they have been observed on the Wednesday, Friday and Saturday in the week before the Third Sunday of Advent, the Second Sunday of Lent, and the Sundays nearest to 29 June and 29 September.

Notes on Collects

For a table showing where the Collects and Post Communions are published, see page 77.

The Collect for each Sunday is used at Evening Prayer on the Saturday preceding, except where that Saturday is a Principal Feast, or a Festival, or the eve of Christmas Day or Easter Day. The Collect for each Sunday is also used on the weekdays following, except where other provision is made.

Where a Collect ends 'through Jesus Christ . . . now and for ever', the minister may omit the longer (trinitarian) ending and use the shorter ending, 'through Jesus Christ our Lord', to which the people respond, 'Amen'. The longer ending, however, is to be preferred at a service of Holy Communion.

Abbreviations used in this book

8

Alt	Alternative	P or p	Purple or Violet
Bp	Bishop	P(La)	Purple or Lent Array
BVM	Blessed Virgin Mary	Ps & Pss	Psalmody
Cant	Canticle	R or r	Red
Comps	Companions	Ss	Saints
DEL	Daily Eucharistic Lectionary	vv	Verses: used where the source is not subdivided into chapters
EP	Evening Prayer	W or w	White (Gold is indicated where its use would be appropriate)
G	Green		

HC Holy Communion: used where additional references are given to provide alternative texts for use at a celebration of Holy Communion (most often the provision of a psalm or gospel)

Mm Martyrs

MP Morning Prayer

Eccles	Ecclesiastes
Ecclus	Ecclesiasticus
Sol	Song of Solomon (also called Song of Songs)

Standard abbreviations have been used for other books of the Bible where necessary.

Alternative dates

The following may be celebrated on the alternative dates indicated:

Chad –
with Cedd on 26 October instead of 2 March

Matthias the Apostle
– on 25 February instead of 14 May

The Visit of the Blessed Virgin Mary to Elizabeth
– on 2 July instead of 31 May

Thomas the Apostle
– on 21 December instead of 3 July

The Blessed Virgin Mary
– on 8 September or 9 September instead of 15 August

If any of these four festivals is celebrated on the alternative date these provisions should be used on the principal date:

Holy Communion	Morning Prayer	Evening Prayer
If Matthias the Apostle is celebrated on Monday 25 February the following provision is used on Tuesday 14 May (W):		
Acts 20.17-27	Psalms 98, 99, 100, 106* (or 103)	Psalm 68 or 107*
Psalm 68.9-10, 18-19	Deuteronomy 31.14-29	Numbers 22.36—23.12
John 17.1-11	1 Samuel 10.1-10; 1 Corinthians 12.1-13; 1 John 3.1-10	Luke 8.1-15
If The Visit of the Blessed Virgin Mary to Elizabeth is celebrated on Tuesday 2 July the following provision is used on Friday 31 May (G):		
Ecclesiasticus 44.1, 9-13 or James 5.9-12	Psalms 17, 19	Psalm 22
Psalm 149.1-5 or 103.1-4, 8-13	Job 11	Joshua 9.3-26
Mark 11.11-26	Romans 6.1-14	Luke 11.29-36
If Thomas the Apostle is celebrated on Friday 21 December the following provision is used on Wednesday 3 July (G):		
Genesis 21.5, 8-20	Psalms 110, 111, 112	Psalm 119.129-152
Psalm 34.1-12	Ezekiel 2.3—3.11	1 Samuel 2.12-26
Matthew 8.28-end	2 Corinthians 2.5-end	Luke 20.1-8
If The Blessed Virgin Mary is celebrated on Sunday 8 or Monday 9 September the following provision is used on Thursday 15 August (G):		
Joshua 3.7-11, 13-17	Psalms 90, 92	Psalm 94
Psalm 114	Proverbs 10.1-12	2 Samuel 7.1-17
Matthew 18.21—19.1	Mark 6.1-13	Acts 7.44-53

Key to the Tables

For guidance on how the options for saying the psalms are expressed typographically, see page 5.

Sundays (and Principal Feasts, other Principal Holy Days, and Festivals)

		Principal Service	3rd Service	2nd Service
Day	*Colour*	Main service of the day:	Shorter Readings,	2nd main Service,
	Sunday / Feast † / *Festival* ††	Holy Communion, Morning Prayer, Evening Prayer, or a Service of the Word	an Office lectionary probably used at Morning Prayer where Holy Communion is the Principal Service	probably used at Evening Prayer; adaptable for Holy Communion

† Principal Feasts and other Principal Holy Days are printed in **bold**.
†† Festivals are printed in roman typeface.

Weekdays

		Holy Communion	Morning Prayer	Evening Prayer
Day	*Colour*	Weekday readings	Psalms and readings for Morning Prayer	Psalms and readings for Evening Prayer
	Lesser Festival ‡* [optional]			
	Commemoration ‡‡ [optional]			

‡ Lesser Festivals are printed in roman typeface, in black.
‡‡ Commemorations are printed in *italics*.
* The ascriptions given to holy men and women in the Calendar (such as martyr; teacher of the faith, etc.) have often been abbreviated in this booklet for reasons of space. The particular ascription given is there to be helpful if needing to choose Collects and readings from Common of the Saints; where several ascriptions are used (e.g. bishop and martyr), traditionally the last ascription given is the most important and therefore the guiding one. The full ascriptions may be found in the Calendar, which is printed in *Common Worship: Times and Seasons* (pages 7–22), *Common Worship: Festivals* (pages 5–20) and *Common Worship: Daily Prayer* (pages 5–16). These incorporate minor corrections made since the publication of the Calendar in *Common Worship: Services and Prayers for the Church of England* (pages 5–16).

	Principal Service	3rd Service	2nd Service
Sunday 2 December *P* **1st Sunday of Advent**	Jeremiah 33.14-16 Psalm 25.1-9 1 Thessalonians 3.9-end Luke 21.25-36	Psalm 44 Isaiah 51.4-11 Romans 13.11-end	Psalm 9 [or 9.1-8] Joel 3.9-end Revelation 14.13—15.4 HC John 3.1-17
	Holy Communion	*Morning Prayer*	*Evening Prayer*
Monday 3 December *P* *Francis Xavier, missionary, 1552*	Isaiah 2.1-5 Psalm 122 Matthew 8.5-11	Psalms **50**, 54 or 1, 2, 3 Isaiah 42.18-end Revelation 19	Psalms 70, **71** or **4**, 7 Isaiah 25.1-9 Matthew 12.1-21
Tuesday 4 December *P* *John of Damascus, monk,* *teacher of the faith, c.749* *Nicholas Ferrar, deacon, founder of the* *Little Gidding Community, 1637*	Isaiah 11.1-10 Psalm 72.1-4, 18-19 Luke 10.21-24	Psalms **80**, 82 or **5**, 6 (8) Isaiah 43.1-13 Revelation 20	Psalms **74**, 75 or **9**, 10* Isaiah 26.1-13 Matthew 12.22-37
Wednesday 5 December *P*	Isaiah 25.6-10*a* Psalm 23 Matthew 15.29-37	Psalms 5, **7** or **119.1-32** Isaiah 43.14-end Revelation 21.1-8	Psalms 76, **77** or **11**, 12, 13 Isaiah 28.1-13 Matthew 12.38-end
Thursday 6 December *Pw* *Nicholas, bishop, c.326* (see p.80)	Isaiah 26.1-6 Psalm 118.18-27*a* Matthew 7.21, 24-27	Psalms **42**, 43 or 14, **15**, 16 Isaiah 44.1-8 Revelation 21.9-21	Psalms **40**, 46 or **18*** Isaiah 28.14-end Matthew 13.1-23
Friday 7 December *Pw* *Ambrose, bishop, teacher of the faith,* *397* (see p.79)	Isaiah 29.17-end Psalm 27.1-4, 16-17 Matthew 9.27-31	Psalms **25**, 26 or 17, **19** Isaiah 44.9-23 Revelation 21.22—22.5	Psalms 16, **17** or **22** Isaiah 29.1-14 Matthew 13.24-43
Saturday 8 December *Pw* *Conception of the Blessed Virgin Mary* (see p.78)	Isaiah 30.19-21, 23-26 Psalm 146.4-9 Matthew 9.35—10.1, 6-8	Psalms **9** (10) or 20, 21, **23** Isaiah 44.24—45.13 Revelation 22.6-end	Psalms **27**, 28 or 24, **25** Isaiah 29.15-end Matthew 13.44-end

		Principal Service	3rd Service	2nd Service
Sunday	**9 December** P **2nd Sunday of Advent**	Baruch 5 or Malachi 3.1–4 *Canticle:* Benedictus Philippians 1.3–11 Luke 3.1–6	Psalm 80 Isaiah 64.1–7 Matthew 11.2–11	Psalms 75 [76] Isaiah 40.1–11 Luke 1.1–25
		Holy Communion	**Morning Prayer**	**Evening Prayer**
Monday	**10 December** P	Isaiah 35 Psalm 85.7–end Luke 5.17–26	Psalm **44** or 27, **30** Isaiah 45.14–end 1 Thessalonians 1	Psalms **144**, 146 or 26, **28**, 29 Isaiah 30.1–18 Matthew 14.1–12
Tuesday	**11 December** P	Isaiah 40.1–11 Psalm 96.1, 10–end Matthew 18.12–14	Psalms **56**, 57 or 32, **36** Isaiah 46 1 Thessalonians 2.1–12	Psalms 11, 12, 13 or **33** Isaiah 30.19–end Matthew 14.13–end
Wednesday	**12 December** Ember Day	Isaiah 40.25–end Psalm 103.8–13 Matthew 11.28–end	Psalms **62**, 63 or **34** Isaiah 47 1 Thessalonians 2.13–end	Psalms **10**, 14 or 119.33–56 Isaiah 31 Matthew 15.1–20
Thursday	**13 December** Pr Lucy, martyr, 304 (see p.78) *Samuel Johnson, moralist, 1784*	Isaiah 41.13–20 Psalm 145.1, 8–13 Matthew 11.11–15	Psalms 53, **54**, 60 or **37*** Isaiah 48.1–11 1 Thessalonians 3	Psalm **73** or 39, **40** Isaiah 32 Matthew 15.21–28
Friday	**14 December** Pw John of the Cross, poet, teacher of the faith, 1591 (see p.79) Ember Day	Isaiah 48.17–19 Psalm 1 Matthew 11.16–19	Psalms 85, **86** or 31 Isaiah 48.12–end 1 Thessalonians 4.1–12	Psalms 82, **90** or **35** Isaiah 33.1–22 Matthew 15.29–end
Saturday	**15 December** P Ember Day	Ecclesiasticus 48.1–4, 9–11 or 2 Kings 2.9–12 Psalm 80.1–4, 18–19 Matthew 17.10–13	Psalm 145 or 41, **42**, 43 Isaiah 49.1–13 1 Thessalonians 4.13–end	Psalms 93, **94** or 45, **46** Isaiah 35 Matthew 16.1–12

11

			Principal Service	3rd Service	2nd Service
			Holy Communion	Morning Prayer	Evening Prayer
Sunday	**16 December** **3rd Sunday of Advent**	*P*	Zephaniah 3.14–end *Canticle:* Isaiah 12.2–end [or Psalm 146.4–end] Philippians 4.4–7 Luke 3.7–18	Psalms 12, 14 Isaiah 25.1–9 1 Corinthians 4.1–5	Psalms 50.1–6 [62] Isaiah 35 Luke 1.57–66 [67–end]
Monday	**17 December** *O Sapientia* *Eglantyne Jebb, social reformer,* *founder of 'Save The Children', 1928*	*P*	Genesis 49.2, 8–10 Psalm 72.1–5, 18–19 Matthew 1.1–17	Psalm **40** or **44** Isaiah 49.14–25 1 Thessalonians 5.1–11	Psalms 25, **26** or **47**, 49 Isaiah 38.1–8, 21–22 Matthew 16.13–end
Tuesday	**18 December**	*P*	Jeremiah 23.5–8 Psalm 72.1–2, 12–13, 18–end Matthew 1.18–24	Psalms **70**, 74 or **48**, 52 Isaiah 50 1 Thessalonians 5.12–end	Psalms **50**, 54 or **50** Isaiah 38.9–20 Matthew 17.1–13
				From Wednesday 19 December until the Epiphany *the seasonal psalmody must be used at Morning and Evening Prayer.*	
Wednesday	**19 December**	*P*	Judges 13.2–7, 24–end Psalm 71.3–8 Luke 1.5–25	Psalms 144, **146** Isaiah 51.1–8 2 Thessalonians 1	Psalms 10, **57** Isaiah 39 Matthew 17.14–21
Thursday	**20 December**	*P*	Isaiah 7.10–14 Psalm 24.1–6 Luke 1.26–38	Psalms **46**, 95 Isaiah 51.9–16 2 Thessalonians 2	Psalms **4**, 9 Zephaniah 1.1—2.3 Matthew 17.22–end
Friday	**21 December**	*P*	Zephaniah 3.14–18 Psalm 33.1–4, 11–12, 20–end Luke 1.39–45	Psalms **121**, 122, 123 Isaiah 51.17–end 2 Thessalonians 3	Psalms 80, **84** Zephaniah 3.1–13 Matthew 18.1–20
Saturday	**22 December**	*P*	1 Samuel 1.24–end Psalm 113 Luke 1.46–56	Psalms **124**, 125, 126, 127 Isaiah 52.1–12 Jude	Psalms 24, **48** Zephaniah 3.14–end Matthew 18.21–end

Advent 4 / Christmas

			Principal Service	3rd Service	2nd Service
Sunday	23 December 4th Sunday of Advent	P	Micah 5.2–5a Canticle: Magnificat or Psalm 80.1–8 Hebrews 10.5–10 Luke 1.39–45 [46–55]	Psalm 144 Isaiah 32.1–8 Revelation 22.6–end	Psalms 123 [131] Isaiah 10.33—11.10 Matthew 1.18–end
Monday	24 December Christmas Eve	P	*Morning Eucharist only:* 2 Samuel 7.1–5, 8–11, 16 Psalm 89.2, 19–27 Acts 13.16–26 Luke 1.67–79	Psalms 45, 113 Isaiah 52.13—end of 53 2 Peter 1.1–15	Psalm 85 Zechariah 2 Revelation 1.1–8
Tuesday	25 December Christmas Day	Gold or W	*Any of the following three sets of Principal Service readings may be used on the evening of Christmas Eve and on Christmas Day. Set III should be used at some point during the celebration.* **Set I** Isaiah 9.2–7 Psalm 96 Titus 2.11–14 Luke 2.1–14 [15–20] **Set II** Isaiah 62.6–end Psalm 97 Titus 3.4–7 Luke 2. [1–7] 8–20 **Set III** Isaiah 52.7–10 Psalm 98 Hebrews 1.1–4 [5–12] John 1.1–14	MP Psalms **110**, 117 Isaiah 62.1–5 Matthew 1.18–end	EP Psalm 8 Isaiah 65.17–25 Philippians 2.5–11 or Luke 2.1–20 *if it has not been used at the principal service of the day*
Wednesday	26 December Stephen, deacon, first martyr	R	2 Chronicles 24.20–22 or Acts 7.51–end Psalm 119.161–168 Acts 7.51–end or Galatians 2.16b–20 Matthew 10.17–22	MP Psalms **13**, 31.1–8, 150 Jeremiah 26.12–15 Acts 6	EP Psalms 57, **86** Genesis 4.1–10 Matthew 23.34–end
Thursday	27 December John, Apostle and Evangelist	W	Exodus 33.7–11a Psalm 117 1 John 1 John 21.19b–end	MP Psalms **21**, 147.13–end Exodus 33.12–end 1 John 2.1–11	EP Psalm **97** Isaiah 6.1–8 1 John 5.1–12
Friday	28 December The Holy Innocents	R	Jeremiah 31.15–17 Psalm 124 1 Corinthians 1.26–29 Matthew 2.13–18	MP Psalms **36**, 146 Baruch 4.21–27 or Genesis 37.13–20 Matthew 18.1–10	EP Psalms 123, **128** Isaiah 49.14–25 Mark 10.13–16

			Holy Communion	Morning Prayer	Evening Prayer
Saturday	29 December Thomas Becket, archbishop, martyr, 1170 (see p.78)	Wr	1 John 2.3–11 Psalm 96.1–4 Luke 2.22–35	Psalms 19, 20 Isaiah 57.15–end John 1.1–18	Psalms 131, **132** Jonah 1 Colossians 1.1–14

Christmas 1

		Principal Service	3rd Service	2nd Service
Sunday	**30 December** W **1st Sunday of Christmas**	1 Samuel 2.18–20, 26 Psalm 148 [or 148.7–end] Colossians 3.12–17 Luke 2.41–end	Psalm 105.1–11 Isaiah 41.21—42.1 1 John 1.1–7	Psalm 132 Isaiah 61 Galatians 3.27—4.7 HC Luke 2.15–21

		Holy Communion	Morning Prayer	Evening Prayer
Monday	**31 December** W *John Wyclif, reformer, 1384*	1 John 2.18–21 Psalm 96.1, 11–end John 1.1–18	Psalm 102 Isaiah 59.15b–end John 1.29–34	Psalms **90**, 148 Jonah 3—4 Colossians 1.24—2.7 or: 1st EP of the Naming and Circumcision of Jesus: Psalm 148; Jeremiah 23.1–6; Colossians 2.8–15

		Principal Service	3rd Service	2nd Service
Tuesday	**1 January** W Naming and Circumcision of Jesus	Numbers 6.22–end Psalm 8 Galatians 4.4–7 Luke 2.15–21	MP Psalms **103**, 150 Genesis 17.1–13 Romans 2.17–end	EP Psalm 115 Deuteronomy 30.[1–10] 11–end Acts 3.1–16

		Holy Communion	Morning Prayer	Evening Prayer
Wednesday	**2 January** W Basil the Great and Gregory of Nazianzus, bishops, teachers of the faith, 379 and 389 (see p.79) *Seraphim, monk, spiritual guide, 1833* *Vedanayagam Samuel Azariah,* *bishop, evangelist, 1945*	1 John 2.22–28 Psalm 98.1–4 John 1.19–28	Psalm **18**.1–30 Isaiah 60.1–12 John 1.35–42	Psalms 45, **46** Ruth 1 Colossians 2.8–end
Thursday	**3 January** W	1 John 2.29—3.6 Psalm 98.2–7 John 1.29–34	Psalms 127, 128, 131 Isaiah 60.13–end John 1.43–end	Psalms **2**, 110 Ruth 2 Colossians 3.1–11
Friday	**4 January** W	1 John 3.7–10 Psalm 98.1, 8–end John 1.35–42	Psalm **89**.1–37 Isaiah 61 John 2.1–12	Psalms 85, **87** Ruth 3 Colossians 3.12—4.1
Saturday	**5 January** W	1 John 3.11–21 Psalm 100 John 1.43–end	Psalms 8, **48** Isaiah 62 John 2.13–end	1st EP of the Epiphany: Psalms 96, **97** Isaiah 49.1–13 John 4.7–26

		Principal Service	3rd Service	2nd Service
Sunday **6 January** Epiphany	Gold or W	Isaiah 60.1–6 Psalm 72.[1–9] 10–15 Ephesians 3.1–12 Matthew 2.1–12	MP Psalms **132**, 113 Jeremiah 31.7–14 John 1.29–34	EP Psalm **98**, 100 Baruch 4.36—end of 5 or Isaiah 60.1–9 John 2.1–11
		Holy Communion	*Morning Prayer*	*Evening Prayer*
Monday **7 January**	W	1 John 3.22—4.6 Psalm 2.7–end Matthew 4.12–17, 23–end	Psalms 99, 147.1–12 or 71 Isaiah 63.7–end 1 John 3	Psalm 118 or **72**, 75 Baruch 1.15—2.10 or Jeremiah 23.1–8 Matthew 20.1–16
Tuesday **8 January**	W	1 John 4.7–10 Psalm 72.1–8 Mark 6.34–44	Psalms **46**, 147.13–end or **73** Isaiah 64 1 John 4.7–end	Psalm **145** or **74** Baruch 2.11–end or Jeremiah 30.1–17 Matthew 20.17–28
Wednesday **9 January**	W	1 John 4.11–18 Psalm 72.1, 10–13 Mark 6.45–52	Psalms 2, **148** or **77** Isaiah 65.1–16 1 John 5.1–12	Psalms **67**, 72 or **119.81–104** Baruch 3.1–8 or Jeremiah 30.18—31.9 Matthew 20.29–end
Thursday **10 January** *William Laud, archbishop, 1645*	W	1 John 4.19—5.4 Psalm 72.1, 17–end Luke 4.14–22	Psalms 97, **149** or **78.1–39*** Isaiah 65.17–end 1 John 5.13–end	Psalms 27, **29** or **78.40–end*** Baruch 3.9—4.4 or Jeremiah 31.10–17 Matthew 23.1–12
Friday **11 January** *Mary Slessor, missionary, 1915*	W	1 John 5.5–13 Psalm 147.13–end Luke 5.12–16	Psalms 98, **150** or **55** Isaiah 66.1–11 2 John	Psalms **93**, 132 or **69** Baruch 4.21–30 or Jeremiah 33.14–end Matthew 23.13–28
Saturday **12 January** *Aelred, abbot, 1167 (see p.81) Benedict Biscop, scholar, 689*	W	1 John 5.14–end Psalm 149.1–5 John 3.22–30	Psalms **96**, 145 or **76**, 79 Isaiah 66.12–23 3 John	Psalms **66**, 110 or 81, **84** Baruch 4.36—end of 5 or Micah 5.2–end Matthew 23.29–end *or:* 1st EP of the Baptism of Christ: Psalm 36; Isaiah 61; Titus 2.11–14; 3.4–7

Baptism of Christ (Epiphany 2)

			Principal Service	3rd Service	2nd Service
Sunday	**13 January** Baptism of Christ 2nd Sunday of Epiphany	Gold or W	Isaiah 43.1–7 Psalm 29 Acts 8.14–17 Luke 3.15–17, 21–22	Psalm 89.19–29 Isaiah 42.1–9 Acts 19.1–7	Psalms 46, 47 Isaiah 55.1–11 Romans 6.1–11 HC Mark 1.4–11
			Holy Communion	*Morning Prayer*	*Evening Prayer*
Monday	**14 January** DEL week 1	W	Hebrews 1.1–6 Psalm 97.1–2, 6–10 Mark 1.14–20	Psalms 2, 110 or 80, 82 Amos 1 1 Corinthians 1.1–17	Psalms 34, 36 or 85, 86 Genesis 1.1–19 Matthew 21.1–17
Tuesday	**15 January**	W	Hebrews 2.5–12 Psalm 8 Mark 1.21–28	Psalms 8, 9 or 87, 89.1–18 Amos 2 1 Corinthians 1.18–end	Psalms 45, 46 or 89.19–end Genesis 1.20—2.3 Matthew 21.18–32
Wednesday	**16 January**	W	Hebrews 2.14–end Psalm 105.1–9 Mark 1.29–39	Psalms 19, 20 or 119.105–128 Amos 3 1 Corinthians 2	Psalms 47, 48 or 91, 93 Genesis 2.4–end Matthew 21.33–end
Thursday	**17 January** Antony of Egypt, hermit, abbot, 356 (see p.81) Charles Gore, bishop, founder of the Community of the Resurrection, 1932	W	Hebrews 3.7–14 Psalm 95.1, 8–end Mark 1.40–end	Psalms 21, 24 or 90, 92 Amos 4 1 Corinthians 3	Psalms 61, 65 or 94 Genesis 3 Matthew 22.1–14
Friday	**18 January** Week of Prayer for Christian Unity: 18–25 January Amy Carmichael, founder of the Dohnavur Fellowship, spiritual writer, 1951	W	Hebrews 4.1–5, 11 Psalm 78.3–8 Mark 2.1–12	Psalms 67, 72 or 88 (95) Amos 5.1–17 1 Corinthians 4	Psalm 68 or 102 Genesis 4.1–16, 25–26 Matthew 22.15–33
Saturday	**19 January** Wulfstan, bishop, 1095 (see p.80)	W	Hebrews 4.12–16 Psalm 19.7–end Mark 2.13–17	Psalms 29, 33 or 96, 97, 100 Amos 5.18–end 1 Corinthians 5	Psalms 84, 85 or 104 Genesis 6.1–10 Matthew 22.34–end

		Principal Service	3rd Service	2nd Service
Sunday	**20 January** W **3rd Sunday of Epiphany**	Isaiah 62.1–5 Psalm 36.5–10 I Corinthians 12.1–11 John 2.1–11	Psalm 145.1–13 Isaiah 49.1–7 Acts 16.11–15	Psalm 96 I Samuel 3.1–20 Ephesians 4.1–16 HC John 1.29–42
		Holy Communion	**Morning Prayer**	**Evening Prayer**
Monday	**21 January** Wr Agnes, child martyr, 304 (see p.78) DEL week 2	Hebrews 5.1–10 Psalm 110.1–4 Mark 2.18–22	Psalms 145, **146** or **98**, 99, 101 Amos 6 I Corinthians 6.1–11	Psalm **71** or **105*** (or 103) Genesis 6.11—7.10 Matthew 24.1–14
Tuesday	**22 January** W *Vincent of Saragossa, deacon, martyr, 304*	Hebrews 6.10–end Psalm 111 Mark 2.23–end	Psalms **132**, 147.1–12 or **106*** (or 103) Amos 7 I Corinthians 6.12–end	Psalm **89**.1–37 or **107*** Genesis 7.11–end Matthew 24.15–28
Wednesday	**23 January** W	Hebrews 7.1–3, 15–17 Psalm 110.1–4 Mark 3.1–6	Psalms **81**, 147.13–end or 110, **111**, 112 Amos 8 I Corinthians 7.1–24	Psalms **97**, 98 or **119**.**129–152** Genesis 8.1–14 Matthew 24.29–end
Thursday	**24 January** W Francis de Sales, bishop, teacher of the faith, 1622 (see p.79)	Hebrews 7.25—8.6 Psalm 40.7–10, 17–end Mark 3.7–12	Psalms **76**, 148 or 113, **115** Amos 9 I Corinthians 7.25–end	Psalms 99, 100, **111** or 114, **116**, 117 Genesis 8.15—9.7 Matthew 25.1–13 *or:* 1st EP of the Conversion of Paul: Psalm 149; Isaiah 49.1–13; Acts 22.3–16
		Principal Service	**3rd Service**	**2nd Service**
Friday	**25 January** W Conversion of Paul	Jeremiah 1.4–10 or Acts 9.1–22 Psalm 67 Acts 9.1–22 or Galatians 1.11–16a Matthew 19.27–end	MP Psalms 66, 147.13–end Ezekiel 3.22–end Philippians 3.1–14	EP Psalm 119.41–56 Ecclesiasticus 39.1–10 or Isaiah 56.1–8 Colossians 1.24—2.7
		Holy Communion	**Morning Prayer**	**Evening Prayer**
Saturday	**26 January** W Timothy and Titus, companions of Paul	Hebrews 9.2–3, 11–14 Psalm 47.1–8 Mark 3.20–21 *Lesser Festival eucharistic lectionary:* Isaiah 61.1–3a; Psalm 100; I Timothy 2.1–8 or Titus 1.1–5; Luke 10.1–9	Psalms **122**, 128, 150 or 120, **121**, 122 Hosea 2.2–17 I Corinthians 9.1–14	Psalms **61**, 66 or **118** Genesis 11.1–9 Matthew 25.31–end

Epiphany 4 / Presentation

		Principal Service	3rd Service	2nd Service
Sunday	**27 January** **4th Sunday of Epiphany** — W	Nehemiah 8.1–3, 5–6, 8–10 Psalm 19 [or 19.1–6] 1 Corinthians 12.12–31a Luke 4.14–21	Psalm 113 Deuteronomy 30.11–15 3 John 1.5–8	Psalm 33 [or 33.1–12] Numbers 9.15–end 1 Corinthians 7.17–24 HC Mark 1.21–28
		Holy Communion	*Morning Prayer*	*Evening Prayer*
Monday	**28 January** Thomas Aquinas, priest, philosopher, teacher of the faith, 1274 (see p.79) DEL week 3 — W	Hebrews 9.15, 24–end Psalm 98.1–7 Mark 3.22–30	Psalms 40, 108 or 123, 124, 125, **126** Hosea 2.18—end of 3 1 Corinthians 9.15–end	Psalms **138**, 144 or **127**, 128, 129 Genesis 11.27—12.9 Matthew 26.1–16
Tuesday	**29 January** — W	Hebrews 10.1–10 Psalm 40.1–4, 7–10 Mark 3.31–35	Psalms 34, **36** or **132**, 133 Hosea 4.1–16 1 Corinthians 10.1–13	Psalm **145** or (134), **135** Genesis 13.2–end Matthew 26.17–35
Wednesday	**30 January** Charles, king and martyr, 1649 (see p.78) — Wr	Hebrews 10.11–18 Psalm 110.1–4 Mark 4.1–20	Psalms 45, **46** or **119.153–end** Hosea 5.1–7 1 Corinthians 10.14—11.1	Psalm 21, **29** or **136** Genesis 14 Matthew 26.36–46
Thursday	**31 January** John Bosco, priest, founder of the Salesian Teaching Order, 1888 — W	Hebrews 10.19–25 Psalm 24.1–6 Mark 4.21–25	Psalms 47, **48** or **143**, 146 Hosea 5.8—6.6 1 Corinthians 11.2–16	Psalms 24, 33 or **138**, 140, 141 Genesis 15 Matthew 26.47–56
Friday	**1 February** Brigid, abbess, c.525 — W	Hebrews 10.32–end Psalm 37.3–6, 40–end Mark 4.26–34	Psalms 61, **65** or 142, **144** Hosea 6.7—7.2 1 Corinthians 11.17–end	Psalm **67**, 77 or **145** Genesis 16 Matthew 26.57–end or: **1st EP of the Presentation:** Psalm 118; 1 Samuel 1.19b–end; Hebrews 4.11–end
		Principal Service	*3rd Service*	*2nd Service*
Saturday	**2 February** **Presentation of Christ in the Temple** (Candlemas) — *Gold or W*	Malachi 3.1–5 Psalm 24.[1–6] 7–end Hebrews 2.14–end Luke 2.22–40	MP Psalms **48**, 146 Exodus 13.1–16 Romans 12.1–5	EP Psalms 122, **132** Haggai 2.1–9 John 2.18–22
	or, if the Presentation is celebrated on Sunday 3 February:			
		Holy Communion	*Morning Prayer*	*Evening Prayer*
Saturday	**2 February** — W	Hebrews 11.1–2, 8–19 *Canticle:* Luke 1.69–73 Mark 4.35–end	Psalm **68** or **147** Hosea 8 1 Corinthians 12.1–11	**1st EP of the Presentation:** Psalm 118 1 Samuel 1.19b–end Hebrews 4.11–end

		Principal Service	3rd Service	2nd Service
Sunday 3 February **Second Sunday before Lent**	G	Genesis 2.4b–9, 15–end Psalm 65 Revelation 4 Luke 8.22–25	Psalm 104.1–26 Job 28.1–11 Acts 14.8–17	Psalm 147 [or 147.13–end] Genesis 1.1—2.3 Matthew 6.25–end
or Sunday 3 February **Presentation of Christ in the Temple** (Candlemas)	Gold or W	Malachi 3.1–5 Psalm 24. [1–6] 7–end Hebrews 2.14–end Luke 2.22–40	MP Psalms **48**, 146 Exodus 13.1–16 Romans 12.1–5	EP Psalms 122, **132** Haggai 2.1–9 John 2.18–22
		Holy Communion	**Morning Prayer**	**Evening Prayer**
Monday 4 February *Gilbert, founder of the Gilbertine Order, 1189* DEL week 4	G	Hebrews 11.32–end Psalm 31.19–end Mark 5.1–20	Psalms 1, 2, 3 Ecclesiastes 7.1–14 John 19.1–16	Psalms **4**, 7 Genesis 29.31—30.24 2 Timothy 4.1–8
Tuesday 5 February	G	Hebrews 12.1–4 Psalm 22.25b–end Mark 5.21–43	Psalms **5**, 6 (8) Ecclesiastes 7.15–end John 19.17–30	Psalms **9**, 10* Genesis 31.1–24 2 Timothy 4.9–end
Wednesday 6 February *Martyrs of Japan, 1597* *Accession of Queen Elizabeth II, 1952* (see p.84)	G	Hebrews 12.4–7, 11–15 Psalm 103.1–2, 13–18 Mark 6.1–6	Psalm 119.**1–32** Ecclesiastes 8 John 19.31–end	Psalms 11, 12, 13 Genesis 31.25—32.2 Titus 1
Thursday 7 February	G	Hebrews 12.18–19, 21–24 Psalm 48.1–3, 8–10 Mark 6.7–13	Psalms 14, **15**, 16 Ecclesiastes 9 John 20.1–10	Psalm 18* Genesis 32.3–30 Titus 2
Friday 8 February	G	Hebrews 13.1–8 Psalm 27.1–6, 9–12 Mark 6.14–29	Psalms 17, **19** Ecclesiastes 11.1–8 John 20.11–18	Psalm **22** Genesis 33.1–17 Titus 3
Saturday 9 February	G	Hebrews 13.15–17, 20–21 Psalm 23 Mark 6.30–34	Psalms 20, 21, **23** Ecclesiastes 11.9–end of 12 John 20.19–end	Psalms **24**, 25 Genesis 35 Philemon

Sunday next before Lent

		Principal Service	3rd Service	2nd Service
Sunday	**10 February** G **Sunday next before Lent**	Exodus 34.29–end Psalm 99 2 Corinthians 3.12—4.2 Luke 9.28–36 [37–43a]	Psalm 2 Exodus 33.17–end 1 John 3.1–3	Psalm 89.1–18 [or 89.5–12] Exodus 3.1–6 John 12.27–36a

		Holy Communion	Morning Prayer	Evening Prayer
Monday	**11 February** G DEL week 5	Genesis 1.1–19 Psalm 104.1, 2, 6–13, 26 Mark 6.53–end	Psalms 27, **30** Jeremiah 1 John 3.1–21	Psalms 26, **28**, 29 Genesis 37.1–11 Galatians 1
Tuesday	**12 February** G	Genesis 1.20—2.4a Psalm 8 Mark 7.1–13	Psalms 32, **36** Jeremiah 2.1–13 John 3.22–end	Psalm **33** Genesis 37.12–end Galatians 2.1–10

		Principal Service	3rd Service	2nd Service
Wednesday	**13 February** P(La) Ash Wednesday	Joel 2.1–2, 12–17 or Isaiah 58.1–12 Psalm 51.1–18 2 Corinthians 5.20b—6.10 Matthew 6.1–6, 16–21 or John 8.1–11	MP Psalm **38** Daniel 9.3–6, 17–19 1 Timothy 6.6–19	EP Psalm **51** [or 102.1–18] Isaiah 1.10–18 Luke 15.11–end

		Holy Communion	Morning Prayer	Evening Prayer
Thursday	**14 February** P(La)w Cyril and Methodius, missionaries, 869 and 885 (see p.81) *Valentine, martyr at Rome, c.269*	Deuteronomy 30.15–end Psalm 1 Luke 9.22–25	Psalm **77** or 37* Jeremiah 2.14–32 John 4.1–26	Psalm **74** or 39, **40** Genesis 39 Galatians 2.11–end
Friday	**15 February** P(La) *Sigfrid, bishop, 1045* *Thomas Bray, priest,* *founder of SPCK and SPG, 1730*	Isaiah 58.1–9a Psalm 51.1–5, 17–18 Matthew 9.14–15	Psalms **3**, 7 or **31** Jeremiah 3.6–22 John 4.27–42	Psalm **31** or **35** Genesis 40 Galatians 3.1–14
Saturday	**16 February** P(La)	Isaiah 58.9b–end Psalm 86.1–7 Luke 5.27–32	Psalm **71** or 41, **42**, 43 Jeremiah 4.1–18 John 4.43–end	Psalm **73** or 45, **46** Genesis 41.1–24 Galatians 3.15–22

Lent 1

		Principal Service	3rd Service	2nd Service
Sunday	**17 February** *P(La)* **1st Sunday of Lent**	Deuteronomy 26.1–11 Psalm 91.1–2, 9–end [or 91.1–11] Romans 10.8b–13 Luke 4.1–13	Psalm 50.1–15 Micah 6.1–8 Luke 5.27–end	Psalm 119.73–88 Jonah 3 Luke 18.9–14
		Holy Communion	*Morning Prayer*	*Evening Prayer*
Monday	**18 February** *P(La)*	Leviticus 19.1–2, 11–18 Psalm 19.7–end Matthew 25.31–end	Psalms 10, **11** or **44** Jeremiah 4.19–end John 5.1–18	Psalms 12, **13**, 14 or **47**, 49 Genesis 41.25–45 Galatians 3.23—4.7
Tuesday	**19 February** *P(La)*	Isaiah 55.10–11 Psalm 34.4–6, 21–22 Matthew 6.7–15	Psalm **44** or **48**, 52 Jeremiah 5.1–19 John 5.19–29	Psalms 46, **49** or **50** Genesis 41.46—42.5 Galatians 4.8–20
Wednesday	**20 February** *P(La)* Ember Day	Jonah 3 Psalm 51.1–5, 17–18 Luke 11.29–32	Psalms **6**, 17 or **119.57–80** Jeremiah 5.20–end John 5.30–end	Psalms 9, **28** or **59**, 60 (67) Genesis 42.6–17 Galatians 4.21—5.1
Thursday	**21 February** *P(La)*	Esther 14.1–5, 12 –14 or Isaiah 55.6–9 Psalm 138 Matthew 7.7–12	Psalms **42**, 43 or 56, **57** (63*) Jeremiah 6.9–21 John 6.1–15	Psalms 137, 138, **142** or 61, **62**, 64 Genesis 42.18–28 Galatians 5.2–15
Friday	**22 February** *P(La)* Ember Day	Ezekiel 18.21–28 Psalm 130 Matthew 5.20–26	Psalm **22** or **51**, 54 Jeremiah 6.22–end John 6.16–27	Psalm 54, **55** or **38** Genesis 42.29–end Galatians 5.16–end
Saturday	**23 February** *P(La)r* Polycarp, bishop, martyr, c.155 (see p.78) Ember Day	Deuteronomy 26.16–end Psalm 119.1–8 Matthew 5.43–end	Psalms 59, **63** or **68** Jeremiah 7.1–20 John 6.27–40	Psalms **4**, 16 or 65, **66** Genesis 43.1–15 Galatians 6

Lent 2

	Principal Service	3rd Service	2nd Service
Sunday 24 February P(La) **2nd Sunday of Lent**	Genesis 15.1–12, 17–18 Psalm 27 Philippians 3.17—4.1 Luke 13.31–end	Psalm 119.161–end Genesis 17.1–7, 15–16 Romans 11.13–24	Psalm 135 (or 135.1–14) Jeremiah 22.1–9, 13–17 Luke 14.27–33
	Holy Communion	*Morning Prayer*	*Evening Prayer*
Monday 25 February P(La)	Daniel 9.4–10 Psalm 79.8–9, 12, 14 Luke 6.36–38	Psalms 26, 32 or 71 Jeremiah 7.21–end John 6.41–51	Psalms 70, 74 or 72.75 Genesis 43.16–end Hebrews 1
Tuesday 26 February P(La)	Isaiah 1.10, 16–20 Psalm 50.8, 16–end Matthew 23.1–12	Psalm 50 or 73 Jeremiah 8.1–15 John 6.52–59	Psalms 52, 53, 54 or 74 Genesis 44.1–17 Hebrews 2.1–9
Wednesday 27 February P(La)w George Herbert, priest, poet, 1633 (see p.80)	Jeremiah 18.18–20 Psalm 31.4–5, 14–18 Matthew 20.17–28	Psalm 35 or 77 Jeremiah 8.18—9.11 John 6.60–end	Psalms 3, 51 or 119.81–104 Genesis 44.18–end Hebrews 2.10–end
Thursday 28 February P(La)	Jeremiah 17.5–10 Psalm 1 Luke 16.19–end	Psalm 34 or 78.1–39* Jeremiah 9.12–24 John 7.1–13	Psalm 71 or 78.40–end* Genesis 45.1–15 Hebrews 3.1–6
1 March P(La)w David, bishop, patron of Wales, c.601 (see p.80)	Genesis 37.3–4, 12–13, 17–28 Psalm 105.16–22 Matthew 21.33–43, 45–46	Psalms 40, 41 or 55 Jeremiah 10.1–16 John 7.14–24	Psalms 6, 38 or 69 Genesis 45.16–end Hebrews 3.7–end
2 March P(La)w Chad, bishop, missionary, 672 (see p.81)	Micah 7.14–15, 18–20 Psalm 103.1–4, 9–12 Luke 15.1–3, 11–end	Psalms 3, 25 or 76.79 Jeremiah 10.17–24 John 7.25–36	Psalms 23, 27 or 81, 84 Genesis 46.1–7, 28–end Hebrews 4.1–13

		Principal Service	3rd Service	2nd Service
Sunday 3 March **3rd Sunday of Lent**	P(La)	Isaiah 55.1–9 Psalm 63.1–9 1 Corinthians 10.1–13 Luke 13.1–9	Psalms 26, 28 Deuteronomy 6.4–9 John 17.1a, 11b–19	Psalms 12, 13 Genesis 28.10–19a John 1.35–end
		Holy Communion	Morning Prayer	Evening Prayer
		The following readings may replace those provided for Holy Communion on any day during the Third Week of Lent: *Exodus 17.1–7; Psalm 95.1–2, 6–end; John 4.5–42*		
Monday 4 March	P(La)	2 Kings 5.1–15 Psalms 42.1–2, 43.1–4 Luke 4.24–30	Psalms **5**, 7 or **80**, 82 Jeremiah 11.1–17 John 7.37–52	Psalms 11, **17** or **85**, 86 Genesis 47.1–27 Hebrews 4.14—5.10
Tuesday 5 March	P(La)	Song of the Three 2, 11–20 or Daniel 2.20–23 Psalm 25.3–10 Matthew 18.21–end	Psalms 6, **9** or 87, **89.1–18** Jeremiah 11.18—12.6 John 7.53—8.11	Psalms 61, 62, **64** or **89.19–end** Genesis 47.28—end of 48 Hebrews 5.11—6.12
Wednesday 6 March	P(La)	Deuteronomy 4.1, 5–9 Psalm 147.13–end Matthew 5.17–19	Psalm 38 or **119.105–128** Jeremiah 13.1–11 John 8.12–30	Psalms 36, **39** or **91**, 93 Genesis 49.1–32 Hebrews 6.13–end
Thursday 7 March Perpetua, Felicity and companions, martyrs, 203 (see p.78)	P(La)r	Jeremiah 7.23–28 Psalm 95.1–2, 6–end Luke 11.14–23	Psalms **56**, 57 or 90, **92** Jeremiah 14 John 8.31–47	Psalms **59**, 60 or **94** Genesis 49.33—end of 50 Hebrews 7.1–10
Friday 8 March Edward King, bishop, 1910 (see p.80) Felix, bishop, 647 Geoffrey Studdert Kennedy, priest, poet, 1929	P(La)w	Hosea 14 Psalm 81.6–10, 13, 16 Mark 12.28–34	Psalm 22 or **88** (95) Jeremiah 15.10–end John 8.48–end	Psalm **69** or 102 Exodus 1.1–14 Hebrews 7.11–end
Saturday 9 March	P(La)	Hosea 5.15—6.6 Psalm 51.1–2, 17–end Luke 18.9–14	Psalm 31 or 96, **97**, 100 Jeremiah 16.10—17.4 John 9.1–17	Psalms 116, 130 or **104** Exodus 1.22—2.10 Hebrews 8

		Principal Service	3rd Service	2nd Service
Sunday	**10 March** *P(La)* **4th Sunday of Lent**	Joshua 5.9–12 Psalm 32 2 Corinthians 5.16–end Luke 15.1–3, 11b–end	Psalms **84**, **85** Genesis 37.3–4, 12–end 1 Peter 2.16–end	Psalm 30 Prayer of Manasseh or Isaiah 40.27—41.13 2 Timothy 4.1–18 HC John 11.17–44

For Mothering Sunday:
Exodus 2.1–10 or 1 Samuel 1.20–end; Psalm 34.11–20 or 127.1–4;
2 Corinthians 1.3–7 or Colossians 3.12–17; Luke 2.33–35 or John 19.25b–27
If the Principal Service readings have been displaced by Mothering Sunday provisions, they may be used at the Second Service.

The following readings may replace those provided for Holy Communion on any day during the Fourth Week of Lent:
Micah 7.7–9; Psalm 27.1, 9–10, 16–17; John 9

		Holy Communion	Morning Prayer	Evening Prayer
Monday	**11 March** *P(La)*	Isaiah 65.17–21 Psalm 30.1–5, 8, 11–end John 4.43–end	Psalms 70, **77** or **98**, 99, 101 Jeremiah 17.5–18 John 9.18–end	Psalms **25**, 28 or **105*** (or 103) Exodus 2.11–22 Hebrews 9.1–14
Tuesday	**12 March** *P(La)*	Ezekiel 47.1–9, 12 Psalm 46.1–8 John 5.1–3, 5–16	Psalms 54, **79** or **106*** (or 103) Jeremiah 18.1–12 John 10.1–10	Psalms **80**, 82 or **107*** Exodus 2.23—3.20 Hebrews 9.15–end
Wednesday	**13 March** *P(La)*	Isaiah 49.8–15 Psalm 145.8–18 John 5.17–30	Psalms 63, **90** or 110, **111**, 112 Jeremiah 18.13–end John 10.11–21	Psalms 52, **91** or **119.129—152** Exodus 4.1–23 Hebrews 10.1–18
Thursday	**14 March** *P(La)*	Exodus 32.7–14 Psalm 106.19–23 John 5.31–end	Psalms 53, **86** or 113, **115** Jeremiah 19.1–13 John 10.22–end	Psalms **94** or 114, **116**, 117 Exodus 4.27—6.1 Hebrews 10.19–25
Friday	**15 March** *P(La)*	Wisdom 2.1, 12–22 or Jeremiah 26.8–11 Psalm 34.15–end John 7.1–2, 10, 25–30	Psalm 102 or **139** Jeremiah 19.14—20.6 John 11.1–16	Psalms 13, **16** or **130**, 131, 137 Exodus 6.2–13 Hebrews 10.26–end
Saturday	**16 March** *P(La)*	Jeremiah 11.18–20 Psalm 7.1–2, 8–10 John 7.40–52	Psalm **32** or 120, **121**, 122 Jeremiah 20.7–end John 11.17–27	Psalms **140**, 141, 142 or **118** Exodus 7.8–end Hebrews 11.1–16

		Principal Service	3rd Service	2nd Service
Sunday	**17 March** **5th Sunday of Lent** *Passiontide begins* P(La)	Isaiah 43.16–21 Psalm 126 Philippians 3.4b–14 John 12.1–8	Psalms 111, 112 Isaiah 35 Romans 7.21—8.4	Psalm 35 (or 35.1–9) 2 Chronicles 35.1–6, 10–16 Luke 22.1–13

		Holy Communion	Morning Prayer	Evening Prayer

The following readings may replace those provided for Holy Communion on any day (except St Joseph's Day) during the Fifth Week of Lent:
2 Kings 4.18–21, 32–37; Psalm 17.1–8, 16; John 11.1–45

		Holy Communion	Morning Prayer	Evening Prayer
Monday	**18 March** *Cyril, bishop, teacher of the faith, 386* P(La)	Susanna 1–9, 15–17, 19–30, 33–62 [or 41b–62] or Joshua 2.1–14 Psalm 23 John 8.1–11	Psalms 73, 121 or 123, 124, 125, **126** Jeremiah 21.1–10 John 11.28–44	Psalms 26, 27 or **127**, 128, 129 Exodus 8.1–19 Hebrews 11.17–31 or: 1st EP of Joseph of Nazareth: Psalm 132; Hosea 11.1–9; Luke 2.41–end

		Principal Service	3rd Service	2nd Service
Tuesday	**19 March** Joseph of Nazareth W	2 Samuel 7.4–16 Psalm 89.26–36 Romans 4.13–18 Matthew 1.18–end	MP Psalms 25, 147.1–12 Isaiah 11.1–10 Matthew 13.54–end	EP Psalms 1, 112 Genesis 50.22–end Matthew 2.13–end

		Holy Communion	Morning Prayer	Evening Prayer
Wednesday	**20 March** *Cuthbert, bishop, missionary, 687* (see p.81) P(La)w	Daniel 3.14–20, 24–25, 28 *Canticle: Bless the Lord* John 8.31–42	Psalms **55**, 124 or **119.153–end** Jeremiah 22.20—23.8 John 12.1–11	Psalms 56, **62** or **136** Exodus 9.1–12 Hebrews 12.3–13
Thursday	**21 March** *Thomas Cranmer, archbishop,* *Reformation martyr, 1556* (see p.78) P(La)r	Genesis 17.3–9 Psalm 105.4–9 John 8.51–end	Psalms **40**, 125 or **143**, 146 Jeremiah 23.9–32 John 12.12–19	Psalms 42, **43** or **138**, 140, 141 Exodus 9.13–end Hebrews 12.14–end
Friday	**22 March** P(La)	Jeremiah 20.10–13 Psalm 18.1–6 John 10.31–end	Psalms **22**, 126 or 142, **144** Jeremiah 24 John 12.20–36a	Psalm **31** or **145** Exodus 10 Hebrews 13.1–16
Saturday	**23 March** P(La)	Ezekiel 37.21–end *Canticle: Jeremiah 31.10–13* or Psalm 121 John 11.45–end	Psalms **23**, 127 or **147** Jeremiah 25.1–14 John 12.36b–end	Psalms **128**, 129, **130** or **148**, 149, 150 Exodus 11 Hebrews 13.17–end

		Principal Service	3rd Service	2nd Service
Sunday	24 March Palm Sunday	R	*Liturgy of the Palms:* Luke 19.28–40 Psalm 118.1–2, 19–end [or 118.19–24]	Psalms 61, 62 Zechariah 9.9–12 1 Corinthians 2.1–12	Psalm 69.1–20 Isaiah 5.1–7 Luke 20.9–19
			Liturgy of the Passion: Isaiah 50.4–9a Psalm 31.9–16 [or 31.9–18] Philippians 2.5–11 Luke 22.14—end of 23 or Luke 23.1–49		
			Holy Communion	Morning Prayer	Evening Prayer
				From the Monday of Holy Week until the Saturday of Easter Week the seasonal psalmody must be used.
Monday	25 March Monday of Holy Week	R	Isaiah 42.1–9 Psalm 36.5–11 Hebrews 9.11–15 John 12.1–11	Psalm 41 Lamentations 1.1–12a Luke 22.1–23	Psalm 25 Lamentations 2.8–19 Colossians 1.18–23
Tuesday	26 March Tuesday of Holy Week	R	Isaiah 49.1–7 Psalm 71.1–14 [or 71.1–8] 1 Corinthians 1.18–31 John 12.20–36	Psalm 27 Lamentations 3.1–18 Luke 22. [24–38] 39–53	Psalm 55.13–24 Lamentations 3.40–51 Galatians 6.11–end
Wednesday	27 March Wednesday of Holy Week	R	Isaiah 50.4–9a Psalm 70 Hebrews 12.1–3 John 13.21–32	Psalm 102 [or 102.1–18] Wisdom 1.16—2.1; 2.12–22 or Jeremiah 11.18–20 Luke 22.54–end	Psalm 88 Isaiah 63.1–9 Revelation 14.18—15.4
Thursday	28 March Maundy Thursday	W	Exodus 12.1–4 [5–10] 11–14 Psalm 116.1, 10–end [or 116.9–end] 1 Corinthians 11.23–26 John 13.1–17, 31b–35	Psalms 42, 43 Leviticus 16.2–24 Luke 23.1–25	Psalm 39 Exodus 11 Ephesians 2.11–18
Friday	29 March Good Friday	*Hangings removed;* R *for the Liturgy*	Isaiah 52.13—end of 53 Psalm 22 [or 22.1–11 or 22.1–21] Hebrews 10.16–25 or Hebrews 4.14–16; 5.7–9 John 18.1—end of 19	Psalm 69 Genesis 22.1–18 A part of John 18 and 19 may be read, if not used at the Principal Service or Hebrews 10.1–10	Psalms 130, 143 Lamentations 5.15–end John 19.38–end or Colossians 1.18–23

		Principal Service	3rd Service	2nd Service
Saturday	**30 March** *Hangings removed*	Job 14.1–14 or Lamentations 3.1–9, 19–24	Psalm 142 Hosea 6.1–6 John 2.18–22	Psalm 116 Job 19.21–27 1 John 5.5–12
	Easter Eve *These readings are for use at services other than the Easter Vigil.*	Psalm 31.1–4, 15–16 [or 31.1–5] 1 Peter 4.1–8 Matthew 27.57–end or John 19.38–end		
Saturday or **Sunday**	**30 March evening** *Gold or W* **31 March morning** *Easter Vigil* *The New Testament readings should be preceded by a minimum of three Old Testament readings.* *The Exodus reading should always be used.*	Genesis 1.1–2.4a Genesis 7.1–5, 11–18; 8.6–18; 9.8–13 Genesis 22.1–18 **Exodus 14.10–end; 15.20–21** Isaiah 55.1–11 Baruch 3.9–15, 32—4.4 or Proverbs 8.1–8, 19–21; 9.4b–6 Ezekiel 36.24–28 Ezekiel 37.1–14 Zephaniah 3.14–end **Romans 6.3–11** Luke 24.1–12	Psalm 136.1–9, 23–end Psalm 46 Psalm 16 *Canticle:* **Exodus 15.1b–13, 17–18** *Canticle:* Isaiah 12.2–end Psalm 19 Psalms 42, 43 Psalm 143 Psalm 98 **Psalm 114**	
Sunday	**31 March** *Gold or W* **Easter Day**	Acts 10.34–43† or Isaiah 65.17–end Psalm 118.1–2, 14–24 [or 118.14–24] 1 Corinthians 15.19–26 or Acts 10.34–43† John 20.1–18 or Luke 24.1–12 † *The reading from Acts must be used as either the first or second reading.*	MP Psalms 114, 117 Ezekiel 47.1–12 John 2.13–22	EP Psalm 105 or 66.1–11 Isaiah 43.1–21 1 Corinthians 15.1–11 or John 20.19–23

27

		Holy Communion	Morning Prayer	Evening Prayer
Monday	**1 April** W Monday of Easter Week	Acts 2.14, 22–32 Psalm 16.1–2, 6–end Matthew 28.8–15	Psalms 111, 117, 146 Song of Solomon 1.9—2.7 Mark 16.1–8	Psalm **135** Exodus 12.1–14 1 Corinthians 15.1–11
Tuesday	**2 April** W Tuesday of Easter Week	Acts 2.36–41 Psalm 33.4–5, 18–end John 20.11–18	Psalms **112**, 147.1–12 Song of Solomon 2.8–end Luke 24.1–12	Psalm **136** Exodus 12.14–36 1 Corinthians 15.12–19
Wednesday	**3 April** W Wednesday of Easter Week	Acts 3.1–10 Psalm 105.1–9 Luke 24.13–35	Psalms **113**, 147.13–end Song of Solomon 3 Matthew 28.16–end	Psalm **105** Exodus 12.37–end 1 Corinthians 15.20–28
Thursday	**4 April** W Thursday of Easter Week	Acts 3.11–end Psalm 8 Luke 24.35–48	Psalms **114**, 148 Song of Solomon 5.2—6.3 Luke 7.11–17	Psalm **106** Exodus 13.1–16 1 Corinthians 15.29–34
Friday	**5 April** W Friday of Easter Week	Acts 4.1–12 Psalm 118.1–4, 22–26 John 21.1–14	Psalms **115**, 149 Song of Solomon 7.10—8.4 Luke 8.41–end	Psalm **107** Exodus 13.17—14.14 1 Corinthians 15.35–50
Saturday	**6 April** W Saturday of Easter Week	Acts 4.13–21 Psalm 118.1–4, 14–21 Mark 16.9–15	Psalms **116**, 150 Song of Solomon 8.5–7 John 11.17–44	Psalm **145** Exodus 14.15–end 1 Corinthians 15.51–end

	Principal Service	3rd Service	2nd Service
Sunday W **7 April** **2nd Sunday of Easter**	[Exodus 14.10-end; 15.20-21] Acts 5.27-32 † Psalm 118.14-end or Psalm 150 Revelation 1.4-8 John 20.19-end † *The reading from Acts must be used as either the first or second reading.*	Psalm 136.1-16 Exodus 12.1-13 1 Peter 1.3-12	Psalm 16 Isaiah 52.13—53.12 or 53.1-6, 9-12 Luke 24.13-35 *or:* **1st EP of the Annunciation of Our Lord to the BVM:** Psalm 85; Wisdom 9.1-12 or Genesis 3.8-15; Galatians 4.1-5
Monday *Gold or W* **8 April** *Annunciation of Our Lord to the Blessed Virgin Mary* *(transferred from 25 March)*	Isaiah 7.10-14 Psalm 40.5-11 Hebrews 10.4-10 Luke 1.26-38	MP Psalms 111, 113 1 Samuel 2.1-10 Romans 5.12-end	EP Psalms 131, 146 Isaiah 52.1-12 Hebrews 2.5-end
	Holy Communion	*Morning Prayer*	*Evening Prayer*
Tuesday W **9 April** *Dietrich Bonhoeffer, Lutheran pastor, martyr, 1945*	Acts 4.32-end Psalm 93 John 3.7-15	Psalms 8, 20, 21 or 5, 6 (8) Deuteronomy 1.19-40 John 20.11-18	Psalm 104 or 9, 10* Exodus 15.22—16.10 Colossians 1.15-end
Wednesday W **10 April** *William Law, priest, spiritual writer, 1761* *(see p.79);* *William of Ockham, friar, philosopher, teacher of the faith, 1347*	Acts 5.17-26 Psalm 34.1-8 John 3.16-21	Psalms 16, 30 or 119.1-32 Deuteronomy 3.18-end John 20.19-end	Psalm 33 or 11, 12, 13 Exodus 16.11-end Colossians 2.1-15
Thursday W **11 April** *George Selwyn, bishop, 1878*	Acts 5.27-33 Psalm 34.1, 15-end John 3.31-end	Psalms 28, 29 or 14, 15, 16 Deuteronomy 4.1-14 John 21.1-14	Psalm 34 or 18* Exodus 17 Colossians 2.16—3.11
Friday W **12 April**	Acts 5.34-42 Psalm 27.1-5, 16-17 John 6.1-15	Psalms 57, 61 or 17, 19 Deuteronomy 4.15-31 John 21.15-19	Psalm 118 or 22 Exodus 18.1-12 Colossians 3.12—4.1
Saturday W **13 April**	Acts 6.1-7 Psalm 33.1-5, 18-19 John 6.16-21	Psalms 63, 84 or 20, 21, 23 Deuteronomy 4.32-40 John 21.20-end	Psalm 66 or 24, 25 Exodus 18.13-end Colossians 4.2-end

		Principal Service	3rd Service	2nd Service
Sunday	**14 April** **3rd Sunday of Easter**	[Zephaniah 3.14–end] Acts 9.1–6 [7–20] † Psalm 30 Revelation 5.11–end John 21.1–19 † *The reading from Acts must be used as either the first or second reading.*	Psalm 80.1–8 Exodus 15.1–2, 9–18 John 10.1–19	Psalm 86 Isaiah 38.9–20 John 11. [17–26] 27–44

		Holy Communion	Morning Prayer	Evening Prayer
Monday	**15 April** W	Acts 6.8–15 Psalm 119.17–24 John 6.22–29	Psalms **96**, 27 or 97, **30** Deuteronomy 5.1–22 Ephesians 1.1–14	Psalms **61**, 65 or 26, **28**, 29 Exodus 19 Luke 1.1–25
Tuesday	**16 April** W *Isabella Gilmore, deaconess, 1923*	Acts 7.51—8.1a Psalm 31.1–5, 16 John 6.30–35	Psalms **98**, 99, 100 or 32, **36** Deuteronomy 5.22–end Ephesians 1.15–end	Psalm **71** or **33** Exodus 20.1–21 Luke 1.26–38
Wednesday	**17 April** W	Acts 8.1b–8 Psalm 66.1–6 John 6.35–40	Psalm **105** or **34** Deuteronomy 6 Ephesians 2.1–10	Psalms 67, **72** or 119.**33–56** Exodus 24 Luke 1.39–56
Thursday	**18 April** W	Acts 8.26–end Psalm 66.7–8, 14–end John 6.44–51	Psalm **136** or **37*** Deuteronomy 7.1–11 Ephesians 2.11–end	Psalm **73** or 39, **40** Exodus 25.1–22 Luke 1.57–end
Friday	**19 April** Wr *Alphege, archbishop, martyr, 1012 (see p.78)*	Acts 9.1–20 Psalm 117 John 6.52–59	Psalm **107** or **31** Deuteronomy 7.12–end Ephesians 3.1–13	Psalm **77** or **35** Exodus 28.1–4a, 29–38 Luke 2.1–20
Saturday	**20 April** W	Acts 9.31–42 Psalm 116.10–15 John 6.60–69	Psalms 108, **110**, 111 or 41, **42**, 43 Deuteronomy 8 Ephesians 3.14–end	Psalms 23, **27** or 45, **46** Exodus 29.1–9 Luke 2.21–40

		Principal Service	3rd Service	2nd Service
Sunday	**21 April** W **4th Sunday of Easter**	[Genesis 7.1–5, 11–18; 8.6–18; 9.8–13] Acts 9.36–end † Psalm 23 Revelation 7.9–end John 10.22–30 † *The reading from Acts must be used as either the first or second reading.*	Psalm 146 1 Kings 17.17–end Luke 7.11–23	Psalms 113, 114 Isaiah 63.7–14 Luke 24.36–49

		Holy Communion	Morning Prayer	Evening Prayer
Monday	**22 April** W	Acts 11.1–18 Psalms 42.1–2, 43.1–4 John 10.1–10 (or 11–18)	Psalm **103** or **44** Deuteronomy 9.1–21 Ephesians 4.1–16	Psalms 112, 113, **114** or **47**, 49 Exodus 32.1–14 Luke 2.41–end *or:* 1st EP of George, martyr; patron of England: Psalms 111, 116; Jeremiah 15.15–end; Hebrews 11.32—12.2

		Principal Service	3rd Service	2nd Service
Tuesday	**23 April** R George, martyr, patron of England, c.304	1 Maccabees 2.59–64 or Revelation 12.7–12 Psalm 126 2 Timothy 2.3–13 John 15.18–21	MP Psalms 5, 146 Joshua 1.1–9 Ephesians 6.10–20	EP Psalms 3, 11 Isaiah 43.1–7 John 15.1–8

		Holy Communion	Morning Prayer	Evening Prayer
Wednesday	**24 April** W Mellitus, bishop, 624 Seven Martyrs of the Melanesian Brotherhood, 2003	Acts 12.24—13.5 Psalm 67 John 12.44–end	Psalm **135** or **119.57–80** Deuteronomy 10.12–end Ephesians 5.1–14	Psalms **47**, 48 or **59**, 60 (67) Exodus 33 Luke 3.15–22 *or:* 1st EP of Mark the Evangelist: Psalm 19; Isaiah 52.7–10; Mark 1.1–15

		Principal Service	3rd Service	2nd Service
Thursday	**25 April** R Mark the Evangelist	Proverbs 15.28–end or Acts 15.35–end Psalm 119.9–16 Ephesians 4.7–16 Mark 13.5–13	MP Psalms 37.23–end, 148 Isaiah 62.6–10 or Ecclesiasticus 51.13–end Acts 12.25—13.13	EP Psalm 45 Ezekiel 1.4–14 2 Timothy 4.1–11

		Holy Communion	Morning Prayer	Evening Prayer
Friday	**26 April** W	Acts 13.26–33 Psalm 2 John 14.1–6	Psalm **33** or **51**, 54 Deuteronomy 12.1–14 Ephesians 6.1–9	Psalms **36**, 40 or **38** Exodus 35.20—36.7 Luke 4.1–30
Saturday	**27 April** W Christina Rossetti, poet, 1894	Acts 13.44–end Psalm 98.1–5 John 14.7–14	Psalm **34** or **68** Deuteronomy 15.1–18 Ephesians 6.10–end	Psalms **84**, 86 or **65**, 66 Exodus 40.17–end Luke 4.31–37

	Principal Service	2nd Service
Sunday 28 April W **5th Sunday of Easter**	[Baruch 3.9–15, 32—4.4 or Genesis 22.1–18] Acts 11.1–18 † Psalm 148 [or 148.1–6] Revelation 21.1–6 John 13.31–35 † *The reading from Acts must be used as either the first or second reading.*	Psalm 98 Daniel 6.[1–5] 6–23 Mark 15.46—16.8

	Holy Communion	Morning Prayer	Evening Prayer
Monday 29 April W Catherine of Siena, teacher of the faith, 1380 (see p.79)	Acts 14.5–18 Psalm 118.1–3, 14–15 John 14.21–26	Psalm 145 or 71 Deuteronomy 16.1–20 1 Peter 1.1–12	Psalm 105 or 72, 75 Numbers 9.15–end; 10.33–end Luke 4.38–end
Tuesday 30 April W *Pandita Mary Ramabai, translator, 1922*	Acts 14.19–end Psalm 145.10–end John 14.27–end	Psalms 19, 147.1–12 or 73 Deuteronomy 17.8–end 1 Peter 1.13–end	Psalms 96, 97 or 74 Numbers 11.1–33 Luke 5.1–11 or: 1st EP of Philip and James, Apostles: Psalm 25; Isaiah 40.27–end; John 12.20–26

	Principal Service	3rd Service	2nd Service
Wednesday 1 May R Philip and James, Apostles	Isaiah 30.15–21 Psalm 119.1–8 Ephesians 1.3–10 John 14.1–14	MP Psalms 139, 146 Proverbs 4.10–18 James 1.1–12	EP Psalm 149 Job 23.1–12 John 1.43–end

	Holy Communion	Morning Prayer	Evening Prayer
Thursday 2 May W Athanasius, bishop, teacher of the faith, 373 (see p.79)	Acts 15.7–21 Psalm 96.1–3, 7–10 John 15.9–11	Psalms 57, 148 or 78.1–39* Deuteronomy 19 1 Peter 2.11–end	Psalm 104 or 78.40–end* Numbers 13.1–3, 17–end Luke 5.27–end
Friday 3 May W	Acts 15.22–31 Psalm 57.8–end John 15.12–17	Psalms 138, 149 or 55 Deuteronomy 21.22—22.8 1 Peter 3.1–12	Psalm 66 or 69 Numbers 14.1–25 Luke 6.1–11
Saturday 4 May W English saints and martyrs of the Reformation Era	Acts 16.1–10 Psalm 100 John 15.18–21 Lesser Festival eucharistic lectionary: Isaiah 43.1–7 or Ecclesiasticus 2.10–17; Psalm 87;	Psalms 146, 150 or 76, 79 Deuteronomy 24.5–end 1 Peter 3.13–end	Psalm 118 or 81, 84 Numbers 14.26–end Luke 6.12–26

		Principal Service	3rd Service	2nd Service
Sunday 5 May **6th Sunday of Easter**	W	[Ezekiel 37.1–14] Acts 16.9–15 † Psalm 67 Revelation 21.10, 22—22.5 John 14.23–29 or John 5.1–9 † *The reading from Acts must be used as either the first or second reading.*	Psalm 40.1–9 Genesis 1.26–28 [29–end] Colossians 3.1–11	Psalms 126, 127 Zephaniah 3.14–end Matthew 28.1–10, 16–end

		Holy Communion	Morning Prayer	Evening Prayer
Monday 6 May Rogation Day	W	Acts 16.11–15 Psalm 149.1–5 John 15.26—16.4	Psalms **65**, 67 or **80**, 82 Deuteronomy 26 1 Peter 4.1–11	Psalms **121**, 122, 123 or **85**, 86 Numbers 16.1–35 Luke 6.27–38
Tuesday 7 May Rogation Day	W	Acts 16.22–34 Psalm 138 John 16.5–11	Psalms 124, 125, **126**, 127 or 87, **89.1–18** Deuteronomy 28.1–14 1 Peter 4.12–end	Psalms **128**, 129, 130, 131 or **89.19–end** Numbers 16.36–end Luke 6.39–end
Wednesday 8 May Julian of Norwich, spiritual writer, c.1417 (see p.81) Rogation Day	W	Acts 17.15, 22—18.1 Psalm 148.1–2, 11–end John 16.12–15	Psalms **132**, 133 or 119.**105–128** Deuteronomy 28.58–end 1 Peter 5	**1st EP of Ascension Day:** Psalms 15, 24 2 Samuel 23.1–5 Colossians 2.20—3.4

		Principal Service	3rd Service	2nd Service
Thursday 9 May Ascension Day	W	Acts 1.1–11 † or Daniel 7.9–14 Psalm 47 or Psalm 93 Ephesians 1.15–end or Acts 1.1–11 † Luke 24.44–end † *The reading from Acts must be used as either the first or second reading.*	MP Psalms 110, 150 Isaiah 52.7–end Hebrews 7. [11–25] 26–end	EP Psalm 8 Song of the Three 29–37 or 2 Kings 2.1–15 Revelation 5 HC Matthew 28.16–end

33

		Holy Communion	Morning Prayer	Evening Prayer
		The nine days after Ascension Day until the eve of Pentecost are observed as days of prayer and preparation for the celebration of the outpouring of the Holy Spirit.	*From 10–18 May, in preparation for the Day of Pentecost, an alternative sequence of daily readings for use at the one of the offices is marked with an asterisk*.*	
Friday	10 May	W	Acts 18.9–18 Psalm 47.1–6 John 16.20–23	Psalms 20, **81** or **88** (95) Deuteronomy 29.2–15 1 John 1.1—2.6 *Exodus 35.30—36.1; Galatians 5.13–end*	Psalm **145** or **102** Numbers 20.1–13 Luke 7.11–17
Saturday	11 May	W	Acts 18.22–end Psalm 47.1–2, 7–end John 16.23–28	Psalms 21, **47** or 96, **97**, 100 Deuteronomy 30 1 John 2.7–17 *Numbers 11.16–17, 24–29; 1 Corinthians 2*	Psalms 84, **85** or **104** Numbers 21.4–9 Luke 7.18–35

	Principal Service	3rd Service	2nd Service
Sunday 12 May W **7th Sunday of Easter** *Sunday after Ascension Day*	[Ezekiel 36.24–28] Acts 16.16–34 † Psalm 97 Revelation 22.12–14, 16–17, 20–end John 17.20–end † *The reading from Acts must be used as either the first or second reading.*	Psalm 99 Deuteronomy 34 Luke 24.44–end or Acts 1.1–8	Psalm 68 (or 68.1–13, 18–19) Isaiah 44.1–8 Ephesians 4.7–16 HC Luke 24.44–end
	Holy Communion	**Morning Prayer**	**Evening Prayer**
Monday 13 May W	Acts 19.1–8 Psalm 68.1–6 John 16.29–end	Psalms 93, 96, 97 or **98**, 99, 101 Deuteronomy 31.1–13 1 John 2.18–end *Numbers 27.15–end; 1 Corinthians 3	Psalm 18 or **105*** (or 103) Numbers 22.1–35 Luke 7.36–end or: 1st EP of Matthias the Apostle: Psalm 147; Isaiah 22.15–22; Philippians 3.13b–4.1
	Principal Service	**3rd Service**	**2nd Service**
Tuesday 14 May R Matthias the Apostle	Isaiah 22.15–end or Acts 1.15–end Psalm 15 Acts 1.15–end or 1 Corinthians 4.1–7 John 15.9–17	MP Psalms 16, 147.1–12 1 Samuel 2.27–35 Acts 2.37–end *1 Samuel 10.1–10; 1 Corinthians 12.1–13	EP Psalm 80 1 Samuel 16.1–13a Matthew 7.15–27
	Holy Communion	**Morning Prayer**	**Evening Prayer**
Wednesday 15 May W	Acts 20.28–end Psalm 68.27–28, 32–end John 17.11–19	Psalms 2, **29** or 110, **111**, 112 Deuteronomy 31.30–32.14 1 John 3.11–end * 1 Kings 19.1–18; Matthew 3.13–end	Psalms 36, **46** or **119.129–152** Numbers 23.1–end Luke 8.16–25
Thursday 16 May W *Caroline Chisholm, social reformer, 1877*	Acts 22.30, 23.6–11 Psalm 16.1, 5–end John 17.20–end	Psalms 24, **72** or 113, **115** Deuteronomy 32.15–47 1 John 4.1–6 *Ezekiel 11.14–20; Matthew 9.35—10.20	Psalm **139** or 114, **116**, 117 Numbers 24 Luke 8.26–39
Friday 17 May W	Acts 25.13–21 Psalm 103.1–2, 11–12, 19–20 John 21.15–19	Psalms 28, **30** or 139 Deuteronomy 33 1 John 4.7–end *Ezekiel 36.22–28; Matthew 12.22–32	Psalm 147 or **130**, 131, 137 Numbers 27.12–end Luke 8.40–end
Saturday 18 May W	Acts 28.16–20, 30–end Psalm 11.4–end John 21.20–end	Psalms 42, **43** or 120, **121**, 122 Deuteronomy 32.48–end, 34 1 John 5 *Micah 3.1–8; Ephesians 6.10–20	**1st EP of Pentecost:** Psalm 48 Deuteronomy 16.9–15 John 7.37–39

	Principal Service	3rd Service	2nd Service
Sunday 19 May **Pentecost** *Whit Sunday* — R	Acts 2.1–21 † or Genesis 11.1–9 Psalm 104.26–36, 37b [104.26–end] Romans 8.14–17 or Acts 2.1–21 † John 14.8–17 [25–27] † *The reading from Acts must be used as either the first or second reading.*	MP Psalms 36.5–10; 150 Isaiah 40.12–23 or Wisdom 9.9–17 1 Corinthians 2.6–end	EP Psalm 33.1–12 Exodus 33.7–20 2 Corinthians 3.4–end HC John 16.4b–15
	Holy Communion	Morning Prayer	Evening Prayer
Monday 20 May Alcuin, deacon, abbot, 804 (see p.81) Ordinary Time resumes today DEL week 7 — Gw	Ecclesiasticus 1.1–10 or James 1.1–11 Psalm 93 or 119.65–72 Mark 9.14–29	Psalms 123, 124, 125, **126** Job 1 Romans 1.1–17	Psalms **127**, 128, 129 Joshua 1 Luke 9.18–27
Tuesday 21 May *Helena, protector of the Holy Places, 330* — G	Ecclesiasticus 2.1–11 or James 1.12–18 Psalm 37.3–6, 27–28 or 94.12–18 Mark 9.30–37	Psalms **132**, 133 Job 2 Romans 1.18–end	Psalms (134,) **135** Joshua 2 Luke 9.28–36
Wednesday 22 May — G	Ecclesiasticus 4.11–19 or James 1.19–end Psalm 119.161–168 or 15 Mark 9.38–40	Psalm **119.153–end** Job 3 Romans 2.1–16	Psalm **136** Joshua 3 Luke 9.37–50
Thursday 23 May — G	Ecclesiasticus 5.1–8 or James 1.1–9 Psalm 1 or 34.1–7 Mark 9.41–end	Psalms **143**, 146 Job 4 Romans 2.17–end	Psalms **138**, 140, 141 Joshua 4.1–5.1 Luke 9.51–end
Friday 24 May John and Charles Wesley, evangelists, hymn writers, 1791 and 1788 (see p.80) — Gw	Ecclesiasticus 6.5–17 or James 2.14–24, 26 Psalm 119.19–24 or 112 Mark 10.1–12	Psalms 142, **144** Job 5 Romans 3.1–20	Psalm **145** Joshua 5.2–end Luke 10.1–16
Saturday 25 May The Venerable Bede, monk, scholar, historian, 735 (see p.81) *Aldhelm, bishop, 709* — Gw	Ecclesiasticus 17.1–15 or James 3.1–10 Psalm 103.13–18 or 12.1–7 Mark 10.13–16	Psalm **147** Job 6 Romans 3.21–end	**1st EP of Trinity Sunday:** Psalms 97, 98 Isaiah 40.12–end Mark 1.1–13

		Principal Service	3rd Service	2nd Service
Sunday **26 May** Trinity Sunday	*Gold or W*	Proverbs 8.1–4, 22–31 Psalm 8 Romans 5.1–5 John 16.12–15	MP Psalm 29 Isaiah 6.1–8 Revelation 4	EP Psalm 73.1–3, 16–end Exodus 3.1–15 John 3.1–17
		Holy Communion	**Morning Prayer**	**Evening Prayer**
Monday **27 May** DEL week 8	G	Ecclesiasticus 17.24–29 or James 3.13–end Psalm 32.1–8 or 19.7–end Mark 10.17–27	Psalms 1, 2, 3 Job 7 Romans 4.1–12	Psalms **4**, 7 Joshua 7.1–15 Luke 10.25–37
Tuesday **28 May** *Lanfranc, monk, archbishop, scholar, 1089*	G	Ecclesiasticus 35.1–12 or James 4.1–10 Psalm 50.1–6 or 55.7–9, 24 Mark 10.28–31	Psalms **5**, 6 (8) Job 8 Romans 4.13–end	Psalms **9**, 10* Joshua 7.16–end Luke 10.38–end
Wednesday **29 May**	G	Ecclesiasticus 36.1–2, 4–5, 10–17 or James 4.13–end Psalm 79.8–9, 12, 14 or 49.1–2, 5–10 Mark 10.32–45	Psalm 119.1–32 Job 9 Romans 5.1–11	Psalms 11, 12, 13 Joshua 8.1–29 Luke 11.1–13 *or:* 1st EP of Corpus Christi: Psalms 110, 111; Exodus 16.2–15; John 6.22–35

	Principal Service	3rd Service	2nd Service
Thursday 30 May W Day of Thanksgiving for the Institution of the Holy Communion (Corpus Christi)	Genesis 14.18–20 Psalm 116.10–end 1 Corinthians 11.23–26 John 6.51–58	MP Psalm 147 Deuteronomy 8.2–16 1 Corinthians 10.1–17	EP Psalms 23, 42, 43 Proverbs 9.1–5 Luke 9.11–17

Alternatively Corpus Christi may be kept as a Lesser Festival, and either these readings or those given below may be used.

	Holy Communion	Morning Prayer	Evening Prayer
Or **Thursday 30 May** Gw Day of Thanksgiving for the Institution of the Holy Communion (Corpus Christi) Josephine Butler, social reformer, 1906 (see p.82) Joan of Arc, visionary, 1431 Apolo Kivebulaya, priest, evangelist, 1933	Ecclesiasticus 42.15–end or James 5.1–6 Psalm 33.1–9 or 49.12–19 Mark 10.46–end	Psalms 14, **15**, 16 Job 10 Romans 5.12–end	Psalm **18*** Joshua 8.30–end Luke 11.14–28 *or:* 1st EP of the Visit of the BVM to Elizabeth: Psalm 45; Song of Solomon 2.8–14; Luke 1.26–38

	Principal Service	3rd Service	2nd Service
Friday 31 May W Visit of the Blessed Virgin Mary to Elizabeth	Zephaniah 3.14–18 Psalm 113 Romans 12.9–16 Luke 1.39–49 [50–56]	MP Psalms 85, 150 1 Samuel 2.1–10 Mark 3.31–end	EP Psalms 122, 127, 128 Zechariah 2.10–end John 3.25–30

	Holy Communion	Morning Prayer	Evening Prayer
Saturday 1 June Gr Justin, martyr, c.165 (see p.78)	Ecclesiasticus 51.12b–20a or James 5.13–end Psalm 19.7–end or 141.1–4 Mark 11.27–end	Psalms 20, 21, **23** Job 12 Romans 6.15–end	Psalms **24**, 25 Joshua 10.1–15 Luke 11.37–end

		Principal Service			3rd Service	2nd Service
Sunday	**2 June** **1st Sunday after Trinity** Proper 4	G	*Continuous:* 1 Kings 18.20, 21 [22–29] 30–39 Psalm 96	*Related:* 1 Kings 8.22–23, 41–43 Psalm 96.1–9	Psalm 41 Deuteronomy 5.1–21 Acts 21.17–39a	Psalm 39 Genesis 4.1–16 Mark 3.7–19
			Galatians 1.1–12 Luke 7.1–10			
		Holy Communion			**Morning Prayer**	**Evening Prayer**
Monday	**3 June** *Martyrs of Uganda, 1885–7, 1977* DEL week 9	G	Tobit 1.1–2, 2.1–8 or 1 Peter 1.3–9 Psalm 15 or 111 Mark 12.1–12		Psalms 27, **30** Job 13 Romans 7.1–6	Psalms 26, **28**, 29 Joshua 14 Luke 12.1–12
Tuesday	**4 June** *Petroc, abbot, 6th cent*	G	Tobit 2.9–end or 1 Peter 1.10–16 Psalm 112 or 98.1–5 Mark 12.13–17		Psalms 32, **36** Job 14 Romans 7.7–end	Psalm **33** Joshua 21.43—22.8 Luke 12.13–21
Wednesday	**5 June** Boniface (Wynfrith), bishop, martyr, 754 (see p.78)	Gr	Tobit 3.1–11, 16–end or 1 Peter 1.18–25 Psalm 25.1–8 or 147.13–end Mark 12.18–27		Psalm **34** Job 15 Romans 8.1–11	Psalm **119.33–56** Joshua 22.9–end Luke 12.22–31
Thursday	**6 June** *Ini Kopuria, founder of the* *Melanesian Brotherhood, 1945*	G	Tobit 6.10–11, 7.1–15, 8.4–8 or 1 Peter 2.2–5, 9–12 Psalm 128 or 100 Mark 12.28–34		Psalm **37*** Job 16.1—17.2 Romans 8.12–17	Psalms 39, **40** Joshua 23 Luke 12.32–40
Friday	**7 June**	G	Tobit 11.5–15 or 1 Peter 4.7–13 Psalm 146 or 96.10–end Mark 12.35–37		Psalm **31** Job 17.3–end Romans 8.18–30	Psalm **35** Joshua 24.1–28 Luke 12.41–48
Saturday	**8 June** Thomas Ken, bishop, nonjuror, hymn writer, 1711 (see p.80)	Gw	Tobit 12.1, 5–15, 20a or Jude 17, 20–25 Psalm 103.1, 8–13 or 63.1–6 Mark 12.38–end		Psalms 41, **42**, 43 Job 18 Romans 8.31–end	Psalms 45, **46** Joshua 24.29–end Luke 12.49–end

Trinity 2

		Principal Service	3rd Service	2nd Service
Sunday 9 June **2nd Sunday after Trinity** Proper 5	G	*Continuous:* 1 Kings 17.8–16 [17–end] Psalm 146 — *Related:* 1 Kings 17.17–end Psalm 30 Galatians 1.11–end Luke 7.11–17	Psalm 45 Deuteronomy 6.10–end Acts 22.22—23.11	Psalm 44 (or 44.1–9) Genesis 8.15—9.17 Mark 4.1–20

		Holy Communion	Morning Prayer	Evening Prayer
Monday 10 June DEL week 10	G	2 Corinthians 1.1–7 Psalm 34.1–8 Matthew 5.1–12	Psalm 44 Job 19 Romans 9.1–18	Psalms **47**, 49 Judges 2 Luke 13.1–9 *or:* 1st EP of Barnabas the Apostle: Psalms 1, 15; Isaiah 42.5–12; Acts 14.8–end

		Principal Service	3rd Service	2nd Service
Tuesday 11 June *Barnabas the Apostle*	R	Job 29.11–16 or Acts 11.19–end Psalm 112 Acts 11.19–end or Galatians 2.1–10 John 15.12–17	MP Psalms 100, 101, 117 Jeremiah 9.23–24 Acts 4.32–end	EP Psalm 147 Ecclesiastes 12.9–end or Tobit 4.5–11 Acts 9.26–31

		Holy Communion	Morning Prayer	Evening Prayer
Wednesday 12 June	G	2 Corinthians 3.4–11 Psalm 78.1–4 Matthew 5.17–19	Psalm **119.57–80** Job 22 Romans 10.1–10	Psalms **59**, 60 (67) Judges 5 Luke 13.22–end
Thursday 13 June	G	2 Corinthians 3.15—4.1, 3–6 Psalm 78.36–40 Matthew 5.20–26	Psalms 56, **57** (63*) Job 23 Romans 10.11–end	Psalms 61, **62**, 64 Judges 6.1–24 Luke 14.1–11
Friday 14 June *Richard Baxter, puritan divine, 1691*	G	2 Corinthians 4.7–15 Psalm 99 Matthew 5.27–32	Psalms **51**, 54 Job 24 Romans 11.1–12	Psalm **38** Judges 6.25–end Luke 14.12–24
Saturday 15 June *Evelyn Underhill, spiritual writer, 1941*	G	2 Corinthians 5.14–end Psalm 103.1–12 Matthew 5.33–37	Psalm **68** Job 25–26 Romans 11.13–24	Psalms 65, **66** Judges 7 Luke 14.25–end

	Principal Service	3rd Service	2nd Service
Sunday G **16 June** **3rd Sunday after Trinity** Proper 6	*Continuous:* 1 Kings 21.1–10 [11–14] 15–21a Psalm 5.1–8 *Related:* 2 Samuel 11.26—12.10, 13–15 Psalm 32 Galatians 2.15–end Luke 7.36—8.3	Psalm 49 Deuteronomy 10.12—11.1 Acts 23.12–end	Psalms 52 [53] Genesis 13 Mark 4.21–end
	Holy Communion	**Morning Prayer**	**Evening Prayer**
Monday G **17 June** *Samuel and Henrietta Barnett,* *social reformers, 1913 and 1936* DEL week 11	2 Corinthians 6.1–10 Psalm 98 Matthew 5.38–42	Psalm **71** Job 27 Romans 11.25–end	Psalms **72**,75 Judges 8.22–end Luke 15.1–10
Tuesday G **18 June** *Bernard Mizeki, martyr, 1896*	2 Corinthians 8.1–9 Psalm 146 Matthew 5.43–end	Psalm **73** Job 28 Romans 12.1–8	Psalm **74** Judges 9.1–21 Luke 15.11–end
Wednesday G **19 June** *Sundar Singh, sadhu (holy man), evangelist,* *teacher of the faith, 1929*	2 Corinthians 9.6–11 Psalm 112 Matthew 6.1–6, 16–18	Psalm **77** Job 29 Romans 12.9–end	Psalm 119.81–**104** Judges 9.22–end Luke 16.1–18
Thursday G **20 June**	2 Corinthians 11.1–11 Psalm 111 Matthew 6.7–15	Psalm **78**.1–39* Job 30 Romans 13.1–7	Psalm **78**.40–end* Judges 11.1–11 Luke 16.19–end
Friday G **21 June**	2 Corinthians 11.18, 21b–30 Psalm 34.1–6 Matthew 6.19–23	Psalm **55** Job 31 Romans 13.8–end	Psalm **69** Judges 11.29–end Luke 17.1–10
Saturday Gr **22 June** *Alban, first martyr of Britain, c.250* (see p.78)	2 Corinthians 12.1–10 Psalm 89.20–33 Matthew 6.24–end	Psalms **76**, 79 Job 32 Romans 14.1–12	Psalms 81, **84** Judges 12.1–7 Luke 17.11–19

Trinity 4

		Principal Service	3rd Service	2nd Service
Sunday 23 June **4th Sunday after Trinity** Proper 7	G	*Continuous:* 1 Kings 19.1–4 [5–7] 8–15a Psalms 42, 43 [or 42 or 43] *Related:* Isaiah 65.1–9 Psalm 22.19–28 Galatians 3.23–end Luke 8.26–39	Psalm 55.1–16, 18–21 Deuteronomy 11.1–15 Acts 27.1–12	Psalms [50] 57 Genesis 24.1–27 Mark 5.21–end or: 1st EP of the Birth of John the Baptist: Psalm 71; Judges 13.2–7, 24–end; Luke 1.5–25
Monday 24 June Birth of John the Baptist	W	Isaiah 40.1–11 Psalm 85.7–end Acts 13.14b–26 or Galatians 3.23–end Luke 1.57–66, 80	*MP* Psalms 50, 149 Ecclesiasticus 48.1–10 or Malachi 3.1–6 Luke 3.1–17	*EP* Psalms 80, 82 Malachi 4 Matthew 11.2–19

		Holy Communion	Morning Prayer	Evening Prayer
Tuesday 25 June DEL week 12	G	Genesis 13.2, 5–end Psalm 15 Matthew 7.6, 12–14	Psalms 87, **89.1–18** Job 38 Romans 15.1–13	Psalm **89.19–end** Judges 14 Luke 18.1–14
Wednesday 26 June Ember Day	G	Genesis 15.1–12, 17–18 Psalm 105.1–9 Matthew 7.15–20	Psalm 119.**105–128** Job 39 Romans 15.14–21	Psalms **91**, 93 Judges 15.1—16.3 Luke 18.15–30
Thursday 27 June *Cyril, bishop, teacher of the faith, 444*	G	Genesis 16.1–12, 15–16 Psalm 106.1–5 Matthew 7.21–end	Psalms 90, **92** Job 40 Romans 15.22–end	Psalm **94** Judges 16.4–end Luke 18.31–end
Friday 28 June *Irenaeus, bishop, teacher of the faith, c.200 (see p.79)* Ember Day	Gw	Genesis 17.1, 9–10, 15–22 Psalm 128 Matthew 8.1–4	Psalms **88** (95) Job 41 Romans 16.1–16 or: 1st EP of Peter and Paul, Apostles [or †Peter the Apostle alone]: Psalms 66, 67; Ezekiel 3.4–11; Galatians 1.13—2.8 [†Acts 9.32–end]	Psalm **102** Judges 17 Luke 19.1–10

		Principal Service	3rd Service	2nd Service
Saturday 29 June Peter and Paul, Apostles or Peter the Apostle Ember Day	R R	*Peter and Paul:* Zechariah 4.1–6a, 10b–end or Acts 12.1–11 Psalm 125 Acts 12.1–11 or 2 Timothy 4.6–8, 17–18 Matthew 16.13–19 *Peter alone:* Ezekiel 3.22–end or Acts 12.1–11 Psalm 125 Acts 12.1–11 or 1 Peter 2.19–end Matthew 16.13–19	*MP* Psalms 71, 113 Isaiah 49.1–6 Acts 11.1–18	*EP* Psalms 124, 138 Ezekiel 34.11–16 John 21.15–22

			Principal Service		3rd Service	2nd Service

Sunday 30 June — G — **5th Sunday after Trinity** — Proper 8

Principal Service	3rd Service	2nd Service
Continuous: 2 Kings 2.1–2, 6–14 Psalm 77.1–2, 11–end [or 77.11–end] *Related:* 1 Kings 19.5–16, 19–end Psalm 16 Galatians 5.1, 13–25 Luke 9.51–end	Psalm 64 Deuteronomy 15.1–11 Acts 27.[13–32] 33–end	Psalms [59.1–6, 18–end] 60 Genesis 27.1–40 Mark 6.1–6

Monday 1 July — G — *Henry, John, and Henry Venn, priests, evangelical divines, 1797, 1813, 1873* — DEL week 13

Holy Communion	Morning Prayer	Evening Prayer
Genesis 18.16–end Psalm 103.6–17 Matthew 8.18–22	Psalms 98, 99, 101 Ezekiel 1.1–14 2 Corinthians 1.1–14	Psalm 105* (or 103) 1 Samuel 1.1–20 Luke 19.28–40

Tuesday 2 July — G

Holy Communion	Morning Prayer	Evening Prayer
Genesis 19.15–29 Psalm 26 Matthew 8.23–27	Psalm 106* (or 103) Ezekiel 1.15—2.2 2 Corinthians 1.15—2.4	Psalm 107* 1 Samuel 1.21—2.11 Luke 19.41–end *or:* 1st EP of Thomas the Apostle: Psalm 27; Isaiah 35; Hebrews 10.35—11.1

Wednesday 3 July — R — Thomas the Apostle

Principal Service	3rd Service	2nd Service
Habakkuk 2.1–4 Psalm 31.1–6 Ephesians 2.19–end John 20.24–29	MP Psalms 92, 146 2 Samuel 15.17–21 or Ecclesiasticus 2 John 11.1–16	EP Psalm 139 Job 42.1–6 1 Peter 1.3–12

Thursday 4 July — G

Holy Communion	Morning Prayer	Evening Prayer
Genesis 22.1–19 Psalm 116.1–7 Matthew 9.1–8	Psalms 113, 115 Ezekiel 3.12–end 2 Corinthians 3	Psalms 114, 116, 117 1 Samuel 2.27–end Luke 20.9–19

Friday 5 July — G

Principal Service	3rd Service	2nd Service
Genesis 23.1–4, 19, 24.1–8, 62–end Psalm 106.1–5 Matthew 9.9–13	Psalm 139 Ezekiel 8 2 Corinthians 4	Psalms 130, 131, 137 1 Samuel 3.1—4.1a Luke 20.20–26

Saturday 6 July — G — *Thomas More, scholar, and John Fisher, bishop, martyrs, 1535*

Principal Service	3rd Service	2nd Service
Genesis 27.1–5a, 15–29 Psalm 135.1–6 Matthew 9.14–17	Psalms 120, 121, 122 Ezekiel 9 2 Corinthians 5	Psalm 118 1 Samuel 4.1b–end Luke 20.27–40

		Principal Service		3rd Service	2nd Service
Sunday	**7 July** G **6th Sunday after Trinity** Proper 9	*Continuous:* 2 Kings 5.1–14 Psalm 30	*Related:* Isaiah 66.10–14 Psalm 66.1–8 Galatians 6.[1–6]7–16 Luke 10.1–11, 16–20	Psalm 74 Deuteronomy 24.10–end Acts 28.1–16	Psalms 65 [70] Genesis 29.1–20 Mark 6.7–29
		Holy Communion		**Morning Prayer**	**Evening Prayer**
Monday	**8 July** DEL week 14	Genesis 28.10–end Psalm 91.1–10 Matthew 9.18–26		Psalms 123, 124, 125, **126** Ezekiel 10.1–19 2 Corinthians 6.1—7.1	Psalms **127**, 128, 129 1 Samuel 5 Luke 20.41—21.4
Tuesday	**9 July** G	Genesis 32.22–end Psalm 17.1–8 Matthew 9.32–end		Psalms **132**, 133 Ezekiel 11.14–end 2 Corinthians 7.2–end	Psalms (134) **135** 1 Samuel 6.1–16 Luke 21.5–19
Wednesday	**10 July** G	Genesis 41.55–end, 42.5–7, 17–end Psalm 33.1–4, 18–end Matthew 10.1–7		Psalm 119.**153–end** Ezekiel 12.1–16 2 Corinthians 8.1–15	Psalm **136** 1 Samuel 7 Luke 21.20–28
Thursday	**11 July** Gw Benedict, abbot, c.550 (see p.81)	Genesis 44.18–21, 23–29, 45.1–5 Psalm 105.11–17 Matthew 10.7–15		Psalms **143**, 146 Ezekiel 12.17–end 2 Corinthians 8.16—9.5	Psalms **138**, 140, 141 1 Samuel 8 Luke 21.29–end
Friday	**12 July** G	Genesis 46.1–7, 28–30 Psalm 37.3–6, 27–28 Matthew 10.16–23		Psalms 142, **144** Ezekiel 13.1–16 2 Corinthians 9.6–end	Psalm **145** 1 Samuel 9.1–14 Luke 22.1–13
Saturday	**13 July** G	Genesis 49.29–end, 50.15–25 Psalm 105.1–7 Matthew 10.24–33		Psalm **147** Ezekiel 14.1–11 2 Corinthians 10	Psalms **148**, 149, 150 1 Samuel 9.15—10.1 Luke 22.14–23

		Principal Service	3rd Service	2nd Service

Sunday	**14 July** G
	7th Sunday after Trinity
	Proper 10
		Continuous:
		Amos 7.7-end
		Psalm 82
		    Related:
		    Deuteronomy 30.9-14
		    Psalm 25.1-10
		Colossians 1.1-14
		Luke 10.25-37
			Psalm 76
			Deuteronomy 28.1-14
			Acts 28.17-end
				Psalm 77 (or 77.1-12)
				Genesis 32.9-30
				Mark 7.1-23

		Holy Communion	**Morning Prayer**	**Evening Prayer**
Monday	**15 July** Gw Swithun, bishop, c.862 (see p.80) *Bonaventure, friar, bishop,* *teacher of the faith, 1274* DEL week 15	Exodus 1.8-14, 22 Psalm 124 Matthew 10.34—11.1	Psalms 1, 2, 3 Ezekiel 14.12-end 2 Corinthians 11.1-15	Psalms **4**, 7 1 Samuel 10.1-16 Luke 22.24-30
Tuesday	**16 July** G *Osmund, bishop, 1099*	Exodus 2.1-15 Psalm 69.1-2, 31-end Matthew 11.20-24	Psalms **5**, 6 (8) Ezekiel 18.1-20 2 Corinthians 11.16-end	Psalms **9**, 10* 1 Samuel 10.17-end Luke 22.31-38
Wednesday	**17 July** G	Exodus 3.1-6, 9-12 Psalm 103.1-7 Matthew 11.25-27	Psalm 119.**1-32** Ezekiel 18.21-32 2 Corinthians 12	Psalms **11**, 12, 13 1 Samuel 11 Luke 22.39-46
Thursday	**18 July** G *Elizabeth Ferard, deaconess, founder of the* *Community of St Andrew, 1883*	Exodus 3.13-20 Psalm 105.1-2, 23 Matthew 11.28-end	Psalms 14, **15**, 16 Ezekiel 20.1-20 2 Corinthians 13	Psalm **18*** 1 Samuel 12 Luke 22.47-62
Friday	**19 July** Gw *Gregory, bishop, and* *his sister Macrina, deaconess,* *teachers of the faith, c.394 and c.379* (see p.79)	Exodus 11.10-12.14 Psalm 116.10-end Matthew 12.1-8	Psalms 17, **19** Ezekiel 20.21-38 James 1.1-11	Psalm 22 1 Samuel 13.5-18 Luke 22.63-end
Saturday	**20 July** G *Margaret of Antioch, martyr, 4th cent.* *Bartolomé de las Casas,* *apostle to the Indies, 1566*	Exodus 12.37-42 Psalm 136.1-4, 10-15 Matthew 12.14-21	Psalms 20, 21, **23** Ezekiel 24.15-end James 1.12-end	Psalms **24**, 25 1 Samuel 13.19—14.15 Luke 23.1-12

Trinity 8

		Principal Service	3rd Service	2nd Service
Sunday	**21 July** G **8th Sunday after Trinity** Proper 11	*Continuous:* Amos 8.1–12 Psalm 52 *Related:* Genesis 18.1–10a Psalm 15 Colossians 1.15–28 Luke 10.38–end	Psalms 82, 100 Deuteronomy 30.1–10 1 Peter 3.8–18	Psalm 81 Genesis 41.1–16, 25–37 1 Corinthians 4.8–13 *or:* 1st EP of Mary Magdalene: Psalm 139; Isaiah 25.1–9; 2 Corinthians 1.3–7
Monday	**22 July** W *Mary Magdalene*	Song of Solomon 3.1–4 Psalm 42.1–10 2 Corinthians 5.14–17 John 20.1–2, 11–18	MP Psalms 30, 32, 150 1 Samuel 16.14–end Luke 8.1–3	EP Psalm 63 Zephaniah 3.14–end Mark 15.40—16.7
		Holy Communion	**Morning Prayer**	**Evening Prayer**
Tuesday	**23 July** G *Bridget, abbess, 1373* DEL week 16	Exodus 14.21—15.1 Psalm 105.37–44 *or Canticle:* Exodus 15.8–10, 12, 17 Matthew 12.46–end	Psalms 32, 36 Ezekiel 33.1–20 James 2.14–end	Psalm 33 1 Samuel 15.1–23 Luke 23.26–43
Wednesday	**24 July** G	Exodus 16.1–5, 9–15 Psalm 78.17–31 Matthew 13.1–9	Psalm 34 Ezekiel 33.21–end James 3	Psalm 119.33–56 1 Samuel 16 Luke 23.44–56a *or:* 1st EP of James the Apostle: Psalm 144; Deuteronomy 30.11–end; Mark 5.21–end
		Principal Service	**3rd Service**	**2nd Service**
Thursday	**25 July** R *James the Apostle*	Jeremiah 45.1–5 or Acts 11.27—12.2 Psalm 126 Acts 11.27—12.2 or 2 Corinthians 4.7–15 Matthew 20.20–28	MP Psalms 7, 29, 117 2 Kings 1.9–15 Luke 9.46–56	EP Psalm 94 Jeremiah 26.1–15 Mark 1.14–20
		Holy Communion	**Morning Prayer**	**Evening Prayer**
Friday	**26 July** Gw *Anne and Joachim, parents of the* *Blessed Virgin Mary*	Exodus 20.1–17 Psalm 19.7–11 Matthew 13.18–23 *Lesser Festival eucharistic lectionary:* Zephaniah 3.14–18a; Psalm 127; Romans 8.28–30; Matthew 13.16–17	Psalm 31 Ezekiel 34.17–end James 4.13—5.6	Psalm 35 1 Samuel 17.31–54 Luke 24.13–35
Saturday	**27 July** G *Brooke Foss Westcott, bishop,* *teacher of the faith, 1901*	Exodus 24.3–8 Psalm 50.1–6, 14–15 Matthew 13.24–30	Psalms 41, **42, 43** Ezekiel 36.1–36 James 5.7–end	Psalms 45, **46** 1 Samuel 17.55—18.16 Luke 24.36–end

		Principal Service		3rd Service	2nd Service
Sunday	**28 July** G **9th Sunday after Trinity** Proper 12	*Continuous:* Hosea 1.2–10 Psalm 85 [or 85.1–7]	*Related:* Genesis 18.20–32 Psalm 138 Colossians 2.6–15 [16–19] Luke 11.1–13	Psalm 95 Song of Solomon 2 or 1 Maccabees 2. [1–14] 15–22 1 Peter 4.7–14	Psalm 88 [or 88.1–10] Genesis 42.1–25 1 Corinthians 10.1–24 HC Matthew 13.24–30 [31–43]
		Holy Communion		Morning Prayer	Evening Prayer
Monday	**29 July** Gw Mary, Martha and Lazarus, companions of Our Lord DEL week 17	Exodus 32.15–24, 30–34 Psalm 106.19–23 Matthew 13.31–35 *Lesser Festival eucharistic lectionary:* Isaiah 25.6–9; Psalm 49.5–10, 16; Hebrews 2.10–15; John 12.1–8		Psalm **44** Ezekiel 37.1–14 Mark 1.1–13	Psalms **47**, 49 1 Samuel 19.1–18 Acts 1.1–14
Tuesday	**30 July** Gw William Wilberforce, social reformer, Olaudah Equiano and Thomas Clarkson, anti-slavery campaigners, 1833, 1797 and 1846 (see p.82)	Exodus 33.7–11, 34.5–9, 28 Psalm 103.8–12 Matthew 13.36–43		Psalms **48**, 52 Ezekiel 37.15–end Mark 1.14–20	Psalm **50** 1 Samuel 20.1–17 Acts 1.15–end
Wednesday	**31 July** G *Ignatius of Loyola, founder of the Society of Jesus, 1556*	Exodus 34.29–end Psalm 99 Matthew 13.44–46		Psalm **119.57–80** Ezekiel 39.21–end Mark 1.21–28	Psalms **59**, 60 (67) 1 Samuel 20.18–end Acts 2.1–21
Thursday	**1 August** G	Exodus 40.16–21, 34–end Psalm 84.1–6 Matthew 13.47–53		Psalms 56, **57** (63*) Ezekiel 43.1–12 Mark 1.29–end	Psalms 61, **62**, 64 1 Samuel 21.1–22.5 Acts 2.22–36
Friday	**2 August** G	Leviticus 23.1, 4–11, 15–16, 27, 34–37 Psalm 81.1–8 Matthew 13.54–end		Psalms **51**, 54 Ezekiel 44.4–16 Mark 2.1–12	Psalm **38** 1 Samuel 22.6–end Acts 2.37–end
Saturday	**3 August** G	Leviticus 25.1, 8–17 Psalm 67 Matthew 14.1–12		Psalm **68** Ezekiel 47.1–12 Mark 2.13–22	Psalms 65, **66** 1 Samuel 23 Acts 3.1–10

		Principal Service	3rd Service	2nd Service
Sunday	**4 August** G **10th Sunday after Trinity** Proper 13	*Continuous:* Hosea 11.1–11 Psalm 107.1–9, 43 [or 107.1–9] *Related:* Ecclesiastes 1.2, 12–14; 2.18–23 Psalm 49.1–12 [or 49.1–9] Colossians 3.1–11 Luke 12.13–21	Psalm 106.1–10 Song of Solomon 5.2–end or 1 Maccabees 3.1–12 2 Peter 1.1–15	Psalm 107.1–32 [or 107.1–12] Genesis 50.4–end 1 Corinthians 14.1–19 HC Mark 6.45–52

		Holy Communion	Morning Prayer	Evening Prayer
Monday	**5 August** Gr Oswald, king, martyr, 642 (see p.78) DEL week 18	Numbers 11.4–15 Psalm 81.1–end Matthew 14.13–21 or 14.22–end	Psalm 71 Proverbs 1.1–19 Mark 2.23–3.6	Psalms 72, 75 1 Samuel 24 Acts 3.11–end or: 1st EP of the Transfiguration of Our Lord: Psalms 99, 110; Exodus 24.12–end; John 12.27–36a

		Principal Service	3rd Service	2nd Service
Tuesday	**6 August** Gold or W Transfiguration of Our Lord	Daniel 7.9–10, 13–14 Psalm 97 2 Peter 1.16–19 Luke 9.28–36	MP Psalms 27, 150 Ecclesiasticus 48.1–10 or 1 Kings 19.1–16 1 John 3.1–3	EP Psalm 72 Exodus 34.29–end 2 Corinthians 3

		Holy Communion	Morning Prayer	Evening Prayer
Wednesday	**7 August** G John Mason Neale, priest, hymn writer, 1866	Numbers 13.1–2, 25—14.1, 26–35 Psalm 106.14–24 Matthew 15.21–28	Psalm 77 Proverbs 2 Mark 3.19b–end	Psalm 119.81–104 1 Samuel 28.3–end Acts 4.13–31

		Principal Service	3rd Service	2nd Service
Thursday	**8 August** Gw Dominic, priest, founder of the Order of Preachers, 1221 (see p.81)	Numbers 20.1–13 Psalm 95.1, 8–end Matthew 16.13–23	Psalm 78.1–39* Proverbs 3.1–26 Mark 4.1–20	Psalm 78.40–end* 1 Samuel 31 Acts 4.32—5.11
Friday	**9 August** Gw Mary Sumner, founder of the Mothers' Union, 1921 (see p.82)	Deuteronomy 4.32–40 Psalm 77.11–end Matthew 16.24–end	Psalm 55 Proverbs 3.27–4.19 Mark 4.21–34	Psalm 69 2 Samuel 1 Acts 5.12–26
Saturday	**10 August** Gr Laurence, deacon, martyr, 258 (see p.78)	Deuteronomy 6.4–13 Psalm 18.1–2, 48–end Matthew 17.14–20	Psalms 76, 79 Proverbs 6.1–19 Mark 4.35–end	Psalms 81, 84 2 Samuel 2.1–11 Acts 5.27–end

	Principal Service	3rd Service	2nd Service
Sunday 11 August G **11th Sunday after Trinity** Proper 14	*Continuous:* Isaiah 1.1, 10–20 Psalm 50.1–8, 23–end [or 50.1–7] *Related:* Genesis 15.1–6 Psalm 33.12–end [or 33.12–end] Hebrews 11.1–3, 8–16 Luke 12.32–40	Psalm 115 Song of Solomon 8.5–7 or 1 Maccabees 14.4–15 2 Peter 3.8–13	Psalms 108 [116] Isaiah 11.10—end of 12 2 Corinthians 1.1–22 HC Mark 7.24–30
	Holy Communion	**Morning Prayer**	**Evening Prayer**
Monday 12 August G DEL week 19	Deuteronomy 10.12–end Psalm 147.13–end Matthew 17.22–end	Psalms 80, 82 Proverbs 8.1–21 Mark 5.1–20	Psalms 85, 86 2 Samuel 3.12–end Acts 6
Tuesday 13 August Gw *Jeremy Taylor, bishop, teacher of the faith, 1667 (see p.79)* *Florence Nightingale, nurse, social reformer, 1910* *Octavia Hill, social reformer, 1912*	Deuteronomy 31.1–8 Psalm 107.1–3, 42–end or *Canticle:* Deuteronomy 32.3–4, 7–9 Matthew 18.1–5, 10, 12–14	Psalms 87, **89.1–18** Proverbs 8.22–end Mark 5.21–34	Psalm **89.19–end** 2 Samuel 5.1–12 Acts 7.1–16
Wednesday 14 August G *Maximilian Kolbe, friar, martyr, 1941*	Deuteronomy 34 Psalm 66.14–end Matthew 18.15–20	Psalm 119.**105–128** Proverbs 9 Mark 5.35–end	Psalms **91**, 93 2 Samuel 6.1–19 Acts 7.17–43 *or:* 1st EP of the Blessed Virgin Mary: Psalm 72; Proverbs 8.22–31; John 19.23–27
	Principal Service	**3rd Service**	**2nd Service**
Thursday 15 August W The Blessed Virgin Mary	Isaiah 61.10–end or Revelation 11.19—12.6, 10 Psalm 45.10–end Galatians 4.4–7 Luke 1.46–55	MP Psalms 98, 138, 147.1–12 Isaiah 7.10–15 Luke 11.27–28	EP Psalm 132 Song of Solomon 2.1–7 Acts 1.6–14
	Holy Communion	**Morning Prayer**	**Evening Prayer**
Friday 16 August G	Joshua 24.1–13 Psalm 136.1–3, 16–22 Matthew 19.3–12	Psalms 88 (95) Proverbs 11.1–12 Mark 6.14–29	Psalm 102 2 Samuel 7.18–end Acts 7.54—8.3
Saturday 17 August G	Joshua 24.14–29 Psalm 16.1, 5–end Matthew 19.13–15	Psalms 96, **97**, 100 Proverbs 12.10–end Mark 6.30–44	Psalm 104 2 Samuel 9 Acts 8.4–25

Trinity 12

		Principal Service	3rd Service	2nd Service
Sunday	**18 August** G **12th Sunday after Trinity** Proper 15	*Continuous:* Isaiah 5.1–7 Psalm 80.1–2, 9–end [or 80.9–end] *Related:* Jeremiah 23.23–29 Psalm 82 Hebrews 11.29—12.2 Luke 12.49–56	Psalm 119.33–48 Jonah 1 or Ecclesiasticus 3.1–15 2 Peter 3.14–end	Psalm 119.17–32 [or 119.17–24] Isaiah 28.9–22 2 Corinthians 8.1–9 HC Matthew 20.1–16
		Holy Communion	Morning Prayer	Evening Prayer
Monday	**19 August** G DEL week 20	Judges 2.11–19 Psalm 106.34–42 Matthew 19.16–22	Psalms **98**, 99, 101 Proverbs 14.31—15.17 Mark 6.45–end	Psalm 105* (or 103) 2 Samuel 11 Acts 8.26–end
Tuesday	**20 August** Gw *Bernard, abbot, teacher of the faith, 1153* *(see p.79)* *William and Catherine Booth, founders of the* *Salvation Army, 1912, 1890*	Judges 6.1–24 Psalm 85.8–end Matthew 19.23–end	Psalm 106* (or 103) Proverbs 15.18–end Mark 7.1–13	Psalm 107* 2 Samuel 12.1–25 Acts 9.1–19a
Wednesday	**21 August** G	Judges 9.6–15 Psalm 21.1–6 Matthew 20.1–16	Psalms 110, **111**, 112 Proverbs 18.10–end Mark 7.14–23	Psalm **119.129–152** 2 Samuel 15.1–12 Acts 9.19b–31
Thursday	**22 August** G	Judges 11.29–end Psalm 40.4–11 Matthew 22.1–14	Psalms 113, **115** Proverbs 20.1–22 Mark 7.24–30	Psalms 114, **116**, 117 2 Samuel 15.13–end Acts 9.32–end
Friday	**23 August** G	Ruth 1.1, 3–6, 14–16, 22 Psalm 146 Matthew 22.34–40	Psalm **139** Proverbs 22.1–16 Mark 7.31–end	Psalms **130**, 131, 137 2 Samuel 16.1–14 Acts 10.1–16 *or:* 1st EP of Bartholomew the Apostle: Psalm 97; Isaiah 61.1–9; 2 Corinthians 6.1–10
		Principal Service	3rd Service	2nd Service
Saturday	**24 August** R Bartholomew the Apostle	Isaiah 43.8–13 or Acts 5.12–16 Psalm 145.1–7 Acts 5.12–16 or 1 Corinthians 4.9–15 Luke 22.24–30	MP Psalms 86, 117 Genesis 28.10–17 John 1.43–end	EP Psalms 91, 116 Ecclesiasticus 39.1–10 or Deuteronomy 18.15–19 Matthew 10.1–22

		Principal Service		3rd Service	2nd Service
Sunday	**25 August** G **13th Sunday after Trinity** Proper 16	*Continuous:* Jeremiah 1.4–10 Psalm 71.1–6	*Related:* Isaiah 58.9b–end Psalm 103.1–6 Hebrews 12.18–end Luke 13.10–17	Psalm 119.73–88 Jonah 2 or Ecclesiasticus 3.17–29 Revelation 1	Psalm 119.49–72 [or 119.49–56] Isaiah 30.8–21 2 Corinthians 9 *HC* Matthew 21.28–32
		Holy Communion		Morning Prayer	Evening Prayer
Monday	**26 August** G DEL week 21	1 Thessalonians 1.1–5, 8–end Psalm 149.1–5 Matthew 23.13–22		Psalms 123, 124, 125, **126** Proverbs 25.1–14 Mark 8.11–21	Psalms **127**, 128, 129 2 Samuel 18.1–18 Acts 10.34–end
Tuesday	**27 August** Gw Monica, mother of Augustine of Hippo, 387 (see p.82)	1 Thessalonians 2.1–8 Psalm 139.1–9 Matthew 23.23–26		Psalms **132**, 133 Proverbs 25.15–end Mark 8.22–26	Psalms (134) **135** 2 Samuel 18.19—19.8a Acts 11.1–18
Wednesday	**28 August** Gw Augustine, bishop, teacher of the faith, 430 (see p.79)	1 Thessalonians 2.9–13 Psalm 126 Matthew 23.27–32		Psalm 119.**153–end** Proverbs 26.12–end Mark 8.27—9.1	Psalm **136** 2 Samuel 19.8b–23 Acts 11.19–end
Thursday	**29 August** Gr Beheading of John the Baptist	1 Thessalonians 3.7–end Psalm 90.13–end Matthew 24.42–end *Lesser Festival eucharistic lectionary:* Jeremiah 1.4–10; Psalm 11; Hebrews 11.32—12.2; Matthew 14.1–12		Psalms **143**, 146 Proverbs 27.1–22 Mark 9.2–13	Psalms **138**, 140, 141 2 Samuel 19.24–end Acts 12.1–17
Friday	**30 August** Gw John Bunyan, spiritual writer, 1688 (see p.79)	1 Thessalonians 4.1–8 Psalm 97 Matthew 25.1–13		Psalms 142, **144** Proverbs 30.1–9, 24–31 Mark 9.14–29	Psalm **145** 2 Samuel 23.1–7 Acts 12.18–end
Saturday	**31 August** Gw Aidan, bishop, missionary, 651 (see p.81)	1 Thessalonians 4.9–12 Psalm 98.1–2, 8–end Matthew 25.14–30		Psalm **147** Proverbs 31.10–end Mark 9.30–37	Psalms 148, 149, 150 2 Samuel 24 Acts 13.1–12

		Principal Service	3rd Service	2nd Service
Sunday	**1 September** G **14th Sunday after Trinity** Proper 17	*Continuous:* Jeremiah 2.4–13 Psalm 81.1, 10–end [or 81.1–11] *Related:* Ecclesiasticus 10.12–18 or Proverbs 25.6–7 Psalm 112 Hebrews 13.1–8, 15–16 Luke 14.1, 7–14	Psalm 119.161–end Jonah 3.1–9 or Ecclesiasticus 11[.7–17] 18–28 Revelation 3.14–22	Psalm 119.81–96 [or 119.81–88] Isaiah 33.13–22 John 3.22–36
		Holy Communion	**Morning Prayer**	**Evening Prayer**
Monday	**2 September** G *Martyrs of Papua New Guinea, 1901, 1942* DEL week 22	1 Thessalonians 4.13–end Psalm 96 Luke 4.16–30	Psalms 1, 2, 3 Wisdom 1 or 1 Chronicles 10.1—11.9 Mark 9.38–end	Psalms **4**, 7 1 Kings 1.5–31 Acts 13.13–43
Tuesday	**3 September** Gw Gregory the Great, bishop, teacher of the faith, 604 (see p.79)	1 Thessalonians 5.1–6, 9–11 Psalm 27.1–8 Luke 4.31–37	Psalms **5**, 6 (8) Wisdom 2 or 1 Chronicles 13 Mark 10.1–16	Psalm **9**, 10* 1 Kings 1.32—2.4; 2.10–12 Acts 13.44—14.7
Wednesday	**4 September** G *Birinus, bishop, 650*	Colossians 1.1–8 Psalm 34.11–18 Luke 4.38–end	Psalm 119.1–32 Wisdom 3.1–9 or 1 Chronicles 15.1—16.3 Mark 10.17–31	Psalms **11**, 12, 13 1 Kings 3 Acts 14.8–end
Thursday	**5 September** G	Colossians 1.9–14 Psalm 98.1–5 Luke 5.1–11	Psalms 14, **15**, 16 Wisdom 4.7–end or 1 Chronicles 17 Mark 10.32–34	Psalm **18*** 1 Kings 4.29—5.12 Acts 15.1–21
Friday	**6 September** G *Allen Gardiner, missionary, founder of the* *South American Mission Society, 1851*	Colossians 1.15–20 Psalm 89.19b–28 Luke 5.33–end	Psalms 17, **19** Wisdom 5.1–16 or 1 Chronicles 21.1—22.1 Mark 10.35–45	Psalm **22** 1 Kings 6.1, 11–28 Acts 15.22–35
Saturday	**7 September** G	Colossians 1.21–23 Psalm 117 Luke 6.1–5	Psalms 20, 21, **23** Wisdom 5.17—6.11 or 1 Chronicles 22.2–end Mark 10.46–end	Psalms **24**, 25 1 Kings 8.1–30 Acts 15.36—16.5

		Principal Service	3rd Service	2nd Service
				Evening Prayer
Sunday	**8 September** **15th Sunday after Trinity** Proper 18	*Continuous:* Jeremiah 18.1–11 Psalm 139.1–5, 12–18 [or 139.1–7] *Related:* Deuteronomy 30.15–end Psalm 1 Philemon vv 1–21 Luke 14.25–33	Psalms 122, 123 Jonah 3.10—end of 4 or Ecclesiasticus 27.30—28.9 Revelation 8.1–5	Psalms [120] 121 Isaiah 43.14—44.5 John 5.30–end

G (Sunday)

If the Festival of the Blessed Virgin Mary is transferred to 8 September, the provision (including 1st EP) for 15 August is used.

		Holy Communion	Morning Prayer	Evening Prayer
Monday	**9 September** *Charles Fuge Lowder, priest, 1880* DEL week 23 G	Colossians 1.24—2.3 Psalm 62.1–7 Luke 6.6–11	Psalms 27, **30** Wisdom 6.12–23 or 1 Chronicles 28.1–10 Mark 11.1–11	Psalms 26, **28**, 29 1 Kings 8.31–62 Acts 16.6–24
Tuesday	**10 September** G	Colossians 2.6–15 Psalm 8 Luke 6.12–19	Psalms 32, **36** Wisdom 7.1–14 or 1 Chronicles 28.11–end Mark 11.12–26	Psalm **33** 1 Kings 8.63—9.9 Acts 16.25–end
Wednesday	**11 September** G	Colossians 3.1–11 Psalm 15 Luke 6.20–26	Psalm **34** Wisdom 7.15—8.4 or 1 Chronicles 29.1–9 Mark 11.27–end	Psalm **119.33–56** 1 Kings 10.1–25 Acts 17.1–15
Thursday	**12 September** G	Colossians 3.12–17 Psalm 149.1–5 Luke 6.27–38	Psalm **37*** Wisdom 8.5–18 or 1 Chronicles 29.10–20 Mark 12.1–12	Psalms 39, **40** 1 Kings 11.1–13 Acts 17.16–end
Friday	**13 September** *John Chrysostom, bishop,* *teacher of the faith, 407* (see p.79) Gw	1 Timothy 1.1–2, 12–14 Psalm 16 Luke 6.39–42	Psalm **31** Wisdom 8.21—end of 9 or 1 Chronicles 29.21–end Mark 12.13–17	Psalm **35** 1 Kings 11.26–end Acts 18.1–21 *or:* 1st EP of Holy Cross Day: Psalm 66; Isaiah 52.13—end of 53; Ephesians 2.11–end

		Principal Service	3rd Service	2nd Service
Saturday	**14 September** *Holy Cross Day* R	Numbers 21.4–9 Psalm 22.23–28 Philippians 2.6–11 John 3.13–17	MP Psalms 2, 8, 146 Genesis 3.1–15 John 12.27–36a	EP Psalms 110, 150 Isaiah 63.1–16 1 Corinthians 1.18–25

		Principal Service		3rd Service	2nd Service
Sunday	**15 September** G 16th Sunday after Trinity Proper 19	*Continuous:* Jeremiah 4.11–12, 22–28 Psalm 14	*Related:* Exodus 32.7–14 Psalm 51.1–11	Psalms 126, 127 Isaiah 44.24—45.8 Revelation 12.1–12	Psalms 124, 125 Isaiah 60 John 6.51–69
		1 Timothy 1.12–17 Luke 15.1–10			

		Holy Communion	Morning Prayer	Evening Prayer
Monday	**16 September** Gw Ninian, bishop, c.432 (see p.81) *Edward Bouverie Pusey, priest, 1882* DEL week 24	1 Timothy 2.1–8 Psalm 28 Luke 7.1–10	Psalm 44 Wisdom 11.21—12.2 or 2 Chronicles 2.1–16 Mark 12.28–34	Psalms 47, 49 1 Kings 12.25—13.10 Acts 19.8–20
Tuesday	**17 September** Gw Hildegard, abbess, visionary, 1179 (see p.00)	1 Timothy 3.1–13 Psalm 101 Luke 7.11–17	Psalms 48, 52 Wisdom 12.12–21 or 2 Chronicles 3 Mark 12.35–end	Psalm 50 1 Kings 13.11–end Acts 19.21–end
Wednesday	**18 September** G	1 Timothy 3.14–end Psalm 111.1–5 Luke 7.31–35	Psalm 119.57–80 Wisdom 13.1–9 or 2 Chronicles 5 Mark 13.1–13	Psalms 59, 60 (67) 1 Kings 17 Acts 20.1–16
Thursday	**19 September** G *Theodore, archbishop, 690*	1 Timothy 4.12–end Psalm 111.6–end Luke 7.36–end	Psalms 56, 57 (63*) Wisdom 16.15—17.1 or 2 Chronicles 6.1–21 Mark 13.14–23	Psalms 61, 62, 64 1 Kings 18.1–20 Acts 20.17–end
Friday	**20 September** Gr John Coleridge Patteson, bishop, and companions, martyrs, 1871 (see p.78)	1 Timothy 6.2b–12 Psalm 49.1–9 Luke 8.1–3	Psalms 51, 54 Wisdom 18.6–19 or 2 Chronicles 6.22–end Mark.13.24–31	Psalm 38 1 Kings 18.21–end Acts 21.1–16 *or:* 1st EP of Matthew, Apostle and Evangelist: Psalm 34; Isaiah 33.13–17; Matthew 6.19–end

		Principal Service	3rd Service	2nd Service
Saturday	**21 September** R Matthew, Apostle and Evangelist	Proverbs 3.13–18 Psalm 119.65–72 2 Corinthians 4.1–6 Matthew 9.9–13	MP Psalms 49, 117 1 Kings 19.15–end 2 Timothy 3.14–end	EP Psalms 119.33–40, 89–96 Ecclesiastes 5.4–12 Matthew 19.16–end

		Principal Service	3rd Service	2nd Service
				Psalms [128] 129
				Ezra 1
				John 7.14-36

Sunday — 22 September — 17th Sunday after Trinity — Proper 20 — G

Principal Service	3rd Service	2nd Service
Continuous: Jeremiah 8.18—9.1; Psalm 79.1-9 — Related: Amos 8.4-7; Psalm 113 — 1 Timothy 2.1-7; Luke 16.1-13	Psalms 130, 131; Isaiah 45.9-22; Revelation 14.1-5	Psalms [128] 129; Ezra 1; John 7.14-36

	Holy Communion	Morning Prayer	Evening Prayer
Monday 23 September — DEL week 25 — G	Ezra 1.1-6; Psalm 126; Luke 8.16-18	Psalm 71; 1 Maccabees 1.1-19 or 2 Chronicles 9.1-12; Mark 14.1-11	Psalms 72, 75; 1 Kings 21.37—22.21; Acts 21.37—22.21
Tuesday 24 September — G	Ezra 6.7-8, 12, 14-20; Psalm 124; Luke 8.19-21	Psalm 73; 1 Maccabees 1.20-40 or 2 Chronicles 10.1—11.4; Mark 14.12-25	Psalm 74; 1 Kings 22.1-28; Acts 22.22—23.11
Wednesday 25 September — Gw — Lancelot Andrewes, bishop, spiritual writer, 1626 (see p.80); Sergei of Radonezh, monastic reformer, teacher of the faith, 1392 — Ember Day	Ezra 9.5-9; Canticle: Song of Tobit or Psalm 103.1-6; Luke 9.1-6	Psalm 77; 1 Maccabees 1.41-end or 2 Chronicles 12; Mark 14.26-42	Psalm 119.81-104; 1 Kings 22.29-45; Acts 23.12-end
Thursday 26 September — G — Wilson Carlile, founder of the Church Army, 1942	Haggai 1.1-8; Psalm 149.1-5; Luke 9.7-9	Psalm 78.1-39*; 1 Maccabees 2.1-28 or 2 Chronicles 13.1—14.1; Mark 14.43-52	Psalm 78.40-end*; 2 Kings 1.2-17; Acts 24.1-23
Friday 27 September — Gw — Vincent de Paul, founder of the Lazarists, 1660 (see p.81) — Ember Day	Haggai 1.15b—2.9; Psalm 43; Luke 9.18-22	Psalm 55; 1 Maccabees 2.29-48 or 2 Chronicles 14.2-end; Mark 14.53-65	Psalm 69; 2 Kings 2.1-18; Acts 24.24—25.12
Saturday 28 September — G — Ember Day	Zechariah 2.1-5, 10-11; Psalm 125 or Canticle: Jeremiah 31.10-13; Luke 9.43b-45	Psalms 76, 79; 1 Maccabees 2.49-end or 2 Chronicles 15.1-15; Mark 14.66-end	Psalms 81, 84; 2 Kings 4.1-37; Acts 25.13-end — or: 1st EP of Michael and All Angels: Psalm 91; 2 Kings 6.8-17; Matthew 18.1-6, 10

Michael and All Angels / Trinity 18

If Michael and All Angels is celebrated on Sunday 29 September:

		Principal Service	3rd Service	2nd Service
Sunday	**29 September** W Michael and All Angels	Genesis 28.10–17 or Revelation 12.7–12 Psalm 103.19–end Revelation 12.7–12 or Hebrews 1.5–end John 1.47–end	MP Psalms 34, 150 Tobit 12.6–end or Daniel 12.1–4 Acts 12.1–11	EP Psalms 138, 148 Daniel 10.4–end Revelation 5

		Holy Communion	Morning Prayer	Evening Prayer
Monday	**30 September** G *Jerome, translator, teacher of the faith, 420* DEL week 26	Zechariah 8.1–8 Psalm 102.12–22 Luke 9.46–50	Psalms 80, 82 1 Maccabees 3.1–26 or 2 Chronicles 17.1–12 Mark 15.1–15	Psalms 85, 86 2 Kings 5 Acts 26.1–23

If Michael and All Angels is celebrated on Monday 30 September:

		Principal Service	3rd Service	2nd Service
Sunday	**29 September** G **18th Sunday after Trinity** Proper 21	*Continuous:* Jeremiah 32.1–3a, 6–15 Psalm 91.1–6, 14–end [91.11–end] *Related:* Amos 6.1a, 4–7 Psalm 146 1 Timothy 6.6–19 Luke 16.19–end	Psalm 132 Isaiah 48.12–end Luke 11.37–end	Psalms 134, 135 [or 135.1–14] Nehemiah 2 John 8.31–38, 48–end *or:* 1st EP of Michael and All Angels: Psalm 91; 2 Kings 6.8–17; Matthew 18.1–6, 10
Monday	**30 September** W Michael and All Angels	Genesis 28.10–17 or Revelation 12.7–12 Psalm 103.19–end Revelation 12.7–12 or Hebrews 1.5–end John 1.47–end	MP Psalms 34, 150 Tobit 12.6–end or Daniel 12.1–4 Acts 12.1–11	EP Psalms 138, 148 Daniel 10.4–end Revelation 5

		Holy Communion	Morning Prayer	Evening Prayer
Tuesday	**1 October** G *Remigius, bishop, 533* *Anthony Ashley Cooper (Earl of Shaftesbury),* *social reformer, 1885*	Zechariah 8.20–end Psalm 87 Luke 9.51–56	Psalms 87, **89.1–18** 1 Maccabees 3.27–41 or 2 Chronicles 18.1–27 Mark 15.16–32	Psalm **89.19–end** 2 Kings 6.1–23 Acts 26.24–end
Wednesday	**2 October** G	Nehemiah 2.1–8 Psalm 137.1–6 Luke 9.57–end	Psalm 1 19.105–128 1 Maccabees 3.42–end or 2 Chronicles 18.28—end of 19 Mark 15.33–41	Psalms **91**, 93 2 Kings 9.1–16 Acts 27.1–26
Thursday	**3 October** G *George Bell, bishop, ecumenist,* *peacemaker, 1958*	Nehemiah 8.1–12 Psalm 19.7–11 Luke 10.1–12	Psalms 90, **92** 1 Maccabees 4.1–25 or 2 Chronicles 20.1–23 Mark 15.42–end	Psalm **94** 2 Kings 9.17–end Acts 27.27–end
Friday	**4 October** Gw *Francis of Assisi, friar, deacon, 1226* *(see p.81)*	Baruch 1.15–end or Deuteronomy 31.7–13 Psalm 79.1–9 Luke 10.13–16	Psalms **88** (95) 1 Maccabees 4.26–35 or 2 Chronicles 22.10—end of 23 Mark 16.1–8	Psalm **102** 2 Kings 12.1–19 Acts 28.1–16
Saturday	**5 October** G	Baruch 4.5–12, 27–29 or Joshua 22.1–6 Psalm 69.33–37 Luke 10.17–24	Psalms 96, **97**, 100 1 Maccabees 4.36–end or 2 Chronicles 24.1–22 Mark 16.9–end	Psalm **104** 2 Kings 17.1–23 Acts 28.17–end

Trinity 19

	Principal Service	3rd Service	2nd Service
Sunday **6 October** **19th Sunday after Trinity** Proper 22	G		
	Continuous: Lamentations 1.1–6 Canticle: Lamentations 3.19–26 or Psalm 137 [or 137.1–6] 2 Timothy 1.1–14 Luke 17.5–10	Psalm 141 Isaiah 49.13–23 Luke 12.1–12	Psalm 142 Nehemiah 5.1–13 John 9
	Related: Habakkuk 1.1–4; 2.1–4 Psalm 37.1–9		

or, if the date of dedication of a church is not known, the Dedication Festival (Gold or W) may be celebrated today or on 27 October, or on a suitable date chosen locally (see p.77).

	Holy Communion	Morning Prayer	Evening Prayer
Monday **7 October** DEL week 27	G	Psalms 98, 99, 101	Psalm 105* (or 103)
	Jonah 1.1—2.2, 10 Canticle: Jonah 2.2–4, 7 or Psalm 69.1–6 Luke 10.25–37	1 Maccabees 6.1–17 or 2 Chronicles 26.1–21 John 13.1–11	2 Kings 17.24–end Philippians 1.1–11
Tuesday **8 October**	G	Psalms 106* (or 103)	Psalm 107*
	Jonah 3 Psalm 130 Luke 10.38–end	1 Maccabees 6.18–47 or 2 Chronicles 28 John 13.12–20	2 Kings 18.1–12 Philippians 1.12–end
Wednesday **9 October** *Denys, bishop, and companions, martyrs, c.250* *Robert Grosseteste, bishop, philosopher, scientist, 1253*	G	Psalms 110, 111, 112	Psalm 119.129–152
	Jonah 4 Psalm 86.1–9 Luke 11.1–4	1 Maccabees 7.1–20 or 2 Chronicles 29.1–19 John 13.21–30	2 Kings 18.13–end Philippians 2.1–13
Thursday **10 October** *Paulinus, bishop, missionary, 644 (see p.81)* *Thomas Traherne, poet, spiritual writer, 1674*	Gw	Psalms 113, 115	Psalms 114, 116, 117
	Malachi 3.13—4.2a Psalm 1 Luke 11.5–13	1 Maccabees 7.21–end or 2 Chronicles 29.20–end John 13.31–end	2 Kings 19.1–19 Philippians 2.14–end
Friday **11 October** *Ethelburga, abbess, 675* *James the Deacon, companion of Paulinus, 7th cent.*	G	Psalm 139	Psalms 130, 131, 137
	Joel 1.3–15, 2.1–2 Psalm 9.1–7 Luke 11.15–26	1 Maccabees 9.1–22 or 2 Chronicles 30 John 14.1–14	2 Kings 19.20–36 Philippians 3.1—4.1
Saturday **12 October** *Wilfrid, bishop, missionary, 709 (see p.81)* *Elizabeth Fry, prison reformer, 1845* *Edith Cavell, nurse, 1915*	Gw	Psalms 120, 121, 122	Psalm 118
	Joel 3.12–end Psalm 97.1, 8–end Luke 11.27–28	1 Maccabees 13.41–end, 14.4–15 or 2 Chronicles 32.1–22 John 14.15–end	2 Kings 20 Philippians 4.2–end

			Principal Service	3rd Service	2nd Service
Sunday	**13 October** **20th Sunday after Trinity** Proper 23	G	*Continuous:* Jeremiah 29.1, 4–7 Psalm 66.1–11 *Related:* 2 Kings 5.1–3, 7–15c Psalm 111 2 Timothy 2.8–15 Luke 17.11–19	Psalm 143 Isaiah 50.4–10 Luke 13.22–30	Psalm 144 Nehemiah 6.1–16 John 15.12–end

			Holy Communion	Morning Prayer	Evening Prayer
Monday	**14 October** DEL week 28	G	Romans 1.1–7 Psalm 98 Luke 11.29–32	Psalms 123, 124, 125, **126** 2 Maccabees 4.7–17 or 2 Chronicles 33.1–13 John 15.1–11	Psalms 127, 128, 129 2 Kings 21.1–18 1 Timothy 1.1–17
Tuesday	**15 October** Teresa of Avila, teacher of the faith, 1582 (see p.00)	Gw	Romans 1.16–25 Psalm 19.1–4 Luke 11.37–41	Psalms **132**, 133 2 Maccabees 6.12–end or 2 Chronicles 34.1–18 John 15.12–17	Psalms (134.) **135** 2 Kings 22.1—23.3 1 Timothy 1.18—end of 2
Wednesday	**16 October** *Nicholas Ridley and Hugh Latimer,* *bishops, martyrs, 1555*	G	Romans 2.1–11 Psalm 62.1–8 Luke 11.42–46	Psalm **119.153–end** 2 Maccabees 7.1–19 or 2 Chronicles 34.19–end John 15.18–end	Psalm 136 2 Kings 23.4–25 1 Timothy 3
Thursday	**17 October** Ignatius, bishop, martyr, c.107 (see p.78)	Gr	Romans 3.21–30 Psalm 130 Luke 11.47–end	Psalms **143**, 146 2 Maccabees 7.20–41 or 2 Chronicles 35.1–19 John 16.1–15	Psalms **138**, 140, 141 2 Kings 23.36—24.17 1 Timothy 4 *or:* 1st EP of Luke the Evangelist: Psalm 33; Hosea 6.1–3; 2 Timothy 3.10–end

			Principal Service	3rd Service	2nd Service
Friday	**18 October** Luke the Evangelist	R	Isaiah 35.3–6 or Acts 16.6–10, 4‌1–44 Psalm 147.1–7 2 Timothy 4.5–17 Luke 10.1–9	MP Psalms 145, 146 Isaiah 55 Luke 1.1–4	EP Psalm 103 Ecclesiasticus 38.1–14 or Isaiah 61.1–6 Colossians 4.7–end

			Holy Communion	Morning Prayer	Evening Prayer
Saturday	**19 October** Henry Martyn, translator, missionary, 1812 (see p.81)	Gw	Romans 4.13, 16–18 Psalm 105.6–10, 41–44 Luke 12.8–12	Psalm **147** Tobit 2 or 2 Chronicles 36.11–end John 16.23–end	Psalms **148**, 149, 150 2 Kings 25.22–end 1 Timothy 5.17–end

	Principal Service	3rd Service	2nd Service
Sunday **20 October** **21st Sunday after Trinity** Proper 24 G	*Continuous:* Jeremiah 31.27–34 Psalm 119.97–104 2 Timothy 3.14—4.5 Luke 18.1–8 *Related:* Genesis 32.22–31 Psalm 121 2 Timothy 3.14—4.5 Luke 18.1–8	Psalm 147 Isaiah 54.1–14 Luke 13.31–end	Psalms [146] 149 Nehemiah 8.9–end John 16.1–11

	Holy Communion	Morning Prayer	Evening Prayer
Monday **21 October** DEL week 29 G	Romans 4.20–end *Canticle:* Benedictus 1–6 Luke 12.13–21	Psalms 1, 2, 3 Tobit 3 or Micah 1.1–9 John 17.1–5	Psalms **4**, 7 Judith 4 or Exodus 22.21–27, 23.1–17 1 Timothy 6.1–10
Tuesday **22 October** G	Romans 5.12, 15, 17–end Psalm 40.7–12 Luke 12.35–38	Psalms **5**, 6 (8) Tobit 4 or Micah 2 John 17.6–19	Psalms **9**, 10* Judith 5.1—6.4 or Exodus 29.38—30.16 1 Timothy 6.11–end
Wednesday **23 October** G	Romans 6.12–18 Psalm 124 Luke 12.39–48	Psalm **119.1–32** Tobit 5.1—6.1a or Micah 3 John 17.20–end	Psalms **11**, 12, 13 Judith 6.10—7.7 or Leviticus 8 2 Timothy 1.1–14
Thursday **24 October** G	Romans 6.19–end Psalm 1 Luke 12.49–53	Psalms 14, **15**, 16 Tobit 6.1b–end or Micah 4.1—5.1 John 18.1–11	Psalm **18*** Judith 7.19–end or Leviticus 9 2 Timothy 1.15—2.13
Friday **25 October** *Crispin and Crispinian, martyrs, c.287* G	Romans 7.18–end Psalm 119.33–40 Luke 12.54–end	Psalms 17, **19** Tobit 7 or Micah 5.2–end John 18.12–27	Psalm **22** Judith 8.9–end or Leviticus 16.2–24 2 Timothy 2.14–end
Saturday **26 October** Alfred, king, scholar, 899 (see p.82) *Cedd, abbot, bishop, 664* Gw	Romans 8.1–11 Psalm 24.1–6 Luke 13.1–9	Psalms 20, 21, **23** Tobit 8 or Micah 6 John 18.28–end	Psalms **24**, 25 Judith 9 or Leviticus 17 2 Timothy 3

		Principal Service	2nd Service	3rd Service
Sunday	**27 October** **Last Sunday after Trinity** Proper 25　G	*Continuous:* Joel 2.23–end Psalm 65 [or 65.1–7] *Related:* Ecclesiasticus 35.12–17 or Jeremiah 14.7–10, 19–end Psalm 84.1–7 2 Timothy 4.6–8, 16–18 Luke 18.9–14	Psalm 119.1–16 Ecclesiastes 11, 12 2 Timothy 2.1–7 HC Matthew 22.34–end *or:* 1st EP of Simon and Jude, Apostles: Psalms 124, 125, 126; Deuteronomy 32.1–4; John 14.15–26	Psalm 119.105–128 Isaiah 59.9–20 Luke 14.1–14

or, if the date of dedication of a church is not known, the Dedication Festival *(Gold or W) may be celebrated today or on 7 October, or on a suitable date chosen locally (see p.77)*

		Principal Service	2nd Service	3rd Service
or Sunday	**27 October** **Bible Sunday**　G	Isaiah 45.22–end Psalm 119.129–136 Romans 15.1–6 Luke 4.16–24	Psalm 119.1–16 Jeremiah 36.9–end Romans 10.5–17 HC Matthew 22.34–40 *or:* 1st EP of Simon and Jude, Apostles: Psalms 124, 125, 126; Deuteronomy 32.1–4; John 14.15–26	Psalm 119.105–128 1 Kings 22.1–17 Romans 15.4–13 or Luke 14.1–14
Monday	**28 October** Simon and Jude, Apostles　R	Isaiah 28.14–16 Psalm 119.89–96 Ephesians 2.19–end John 15.17–end	EP Psalm 119.1–16 1 Maccabees 2.42–66 or Jeremiah 3.11–18 Jude vv1–4, 17–end	MP Psalms 116, 117 Wisdom 5.1–16 or Isaiah 45.18–end Luke 6.12–16

		Holy Communion	Evening Prayer	Morning Prayer
Tuesday	**29 October** James Hannington, bishop, martyr, 1885 (see p.78) DEL week 30　Gr	Romans 8.18–25 Psalm 126 Luke 13.18–21	Psalm 33 Judith 11 or Leviticus 23.1–22 2 Timothy 4.9–end	Psalms 32, 36 Tobit 10 or Micah 7.8–end John 19.17–30
Wednesday	**30 October**　G	Romans 8.26–30 Psalm 13 Luke 13.22–30	Psalm 119.33–56 Judith 12 or Leviticus 23.23–end Titus 1	Psalm 34 Tobit 11 or Habakkuk 1.1–11 John 19.31–end
Thursday	**31 October** *Martin Luther, reformer, 1546*　G	Romans 8.31–end Psalm 109.20–26, 29–30 Luke 13.31–end	Psalms 39, **40** Judith 13 or Leviticus 24.1–9 Titus 2	Psalm 37* Tobit 12 or Habakkuk 1.12—2.5 John 20.1–10

or, if All Saints' Day *is celebrated on Thursday 1 November only:*
1st EP of All Saints' Day:
Psalms 1, 5; Ecclesiasticus 44.1–15 or Isaiah 40.27–end;
Revelation 19.6–10

All Saints' Day

All Saints' Day is celebrated either on Friday 1 November or Sunday 3 November; if the latter there may be a supplementary celebration on 1 November.

		Principal Service	3rd Service	2nd Service
Friday	**1 November** All Saints' Day	*Gold or W*	Daniel 7.1–3, 15–18 Psalm 149 Ephesians 1.11–end Luke 6.20–31	MP Psalms 15, **84**, 149 Isaiah 35.1–9 Luke 9.18–27	EP Psalms **148**, 150 Isaiah 65.17–end Hebrews 11.32—12.2

If All Saints' Day is celebrated on Friday 1 November in addition to Sunday 3 November:

			Principal Service	3rd Service	2nd Service
Or **Friday**	**1 November** All Saints' Day	*Gold or W*	Isaiah 56.3–8 or 2 Esdras 2.42–end Psalm 33.1–5 Hebrews 12.18–24 Matthew 5.1–12	MP Psalms 111, **112**, 117 Wisdom 5.1–16 or Jeremiah 31.31–34 2 Corinthians 4.5–12	EP Psalm 145 Isaiah 66.20–23 Colossians 1.9–14

If All Saints' Day is celebrated on Sunday 3 November only:

			Holy Communion	Morning Prayer	Evening Prayer
Or **Friday**	**1 November**	G	Romans 9.1–5 Psalm 147.13–end Luke 14.1–6	Psalm **31** Tobit 13.1–14.1 or Habakkuk 2.6–end John 20.11–18	Psalm **35** Judith 15.1–13 or Leviticus 25.1–24 Titus 3
Saturday	**2 November** Commemoration of the Faithful Departed (All Souls' Day)	Gp	Romans 11.1–2, 11–12, 25–29 Psalm 94.14–19 Luke 14.1, 7–11 *Lesser Festival eucharistic lectionary:* Lamentations 3.17–26, 31–33 or Wisdom 3.1–9; Psalm 23 or 27.1–6, 16–end; Romans 5.5–11 or 1 Peter 1.3–9; John 5.19–25 or John 6.37–40	Psalms 41, **42**, 43 Tobit 14.2–end or Habakkuk 3.2–19a John 20.19–end	Psalms 45, **46** Judith 15.14–end of 16 or Numbers 6.1–5, 21–end Philemon *or where All Saints' Day is celebrated on Sunday 3 November only:* **1st EP of All Saints' Day:** Psalms 1, 5; Ecclesiasticus 44.1–15 or Isaiah 40.27–end; Revelation 19.6–10

4 before Advent / All Saints' Day

If All Saints' Day is celebrated on Thursday 1 November:

		Principal Service	3rd Service	2nd Service
Sunday	**3 November** *R/G* **4th Sunday before Advent**	Isaiah 1.10–18; Psalm 32.1–8; 2 Thessalonians 1; Luke 19.1–10	Psalm 87; Job 26; Colossians 1.9–14	Psalm 145 [or 145.1–9]; Lamentations 3.22–33; John 11.[1–31] 32–44

If All Saints' Day is celebrated on Sunday 3 November only:

		Principal Service	3rd Service	2nd Service
or Sunday	**3 November** **All Saints' Day** *Gold or W*	Daniel 7.1–3, 15–18; Psalm 149; Ephesians 1.1–end; Luke 6.20–31	MP Psalms 15, 84, 149; Isaiah 35.1–9; Luke 9.18–27	EP Psalms 148, 150; Isaiah 65.17–end; Hebrews 11.32—12.2

		Holy Communion	Morning Prayer	Evening Prayer
Monday	**4 November** *R/G* DEL week 31	Romans 11.29–end; Psalm 69.31–37; Luke 14.12–14	Psalms 2, 146 or 44; Isaiah 1.1–20; Matthew 1.18–end	Psalms 92, 96, 97 or 47, 49; Daniel 1; Revelation 1
Tuesday	**5 November** *R/G*	Romans 12.5–16; Psalm 131; Luke 14.15–24	Psalms 5, 147.1–12 or 48, 52; Isaiah 1.21–end; Matthew 2.1–15	Psalms 98, 99, 100 or 50; Daniel 2.1–24; Revelation 2.1–11
Wednesday	**6 November** *R/G* Leonard, hermit, 6th cent. William Temple, archbishop, *teacher of the faith, 1944*	Romans 13.8–10; Psalm 112; Luke 14.25–33	Psalms 9, 147.13–end or 119.57–80; Isaiah 2.1–11; Matthew 2.16–end	Psalms 111, 112, 116 or 59, 60 (67); Daniel 2.25–end; Revelation 2.12–end
Thursday	**7 November** *Rw/Gw* Willibrord, bishop, 739 (see p.81)	Romans 14.7–12; Psalm 27.14–end; Luke 15.1–10	Psalms 11, 15, 148 or 56, 57 (63*); Isaiah 2.12–end; Matthew 3	Psalms 118 or 61, 62, 64; Daniel 3.1–18; Revelation 3.1–13
Friday	**8 November** *Rw/Gw* Saints and martyrs of England	Romans 15.14–21; Psalm 98; Luke 16.1–8; *Lesser Festival eucharistic lectionary:* Isaiah 61.4–9 or Ecclesiasticus 44.1–15; Psalm 15; Revelation 19.5–10; John 17.18–23	Psalms 16, 149 or 51, 54; Isaiah 3.1–15; Matthew 4.1–11	Psalms 137, 138, 143 or 38; Daniel 3.19–end; Revelation 3.14–end
Saturday	**9 November** *R/G* Margery Kempe, mystic, c.1440	Romans 16.3–9, 16, 22–end; Psalm 145.1–7; Luke 16.9–15	Psalms 18.31–end, 150 or 68; Isaiah 4.2—5.7; Matthew 4.12–22	Psalm 145 or 65, 66; Daniel 4.1–18; Revelation 4

		Principal Service	3rd Service	2nd Service
				Psalm 40
Sunday	**10 November** *R/G* **3rd Sunday before Advent** *Remembrance Sunday*	Job 19.23–27a Psalm 17.1–9 [or 17.1–8] 2 Thessalonians 2.1–5, 13–end Luke 20.27–38	Psalms 20, 90 Isaiah 2.1–5 James 3.13–end	1 Kings 3.1–15 Romans 8.31–end HC Matthew 22.15–22
		Holy Communion	Morning Prayer	Evening Prayer
Monday	**11 November** *Rw/Gw* Martin, bishop, c.397 (see p.80) DEL week 32	Wisdom 1.1–7 or Titus 1.1–9 Psalm 139.1–9 or 24.1–6 Luke 17.1–6	Psalms 19, **20** or **71** Isaiah 5.8–24 Matthew 4.23—5.12	Psalm **34** or **72**, 75 Daniel 4.19–end Revelation 5
Tuesday	**12 November** *R/G*	Wisdom 2.23—3.9 or Titus 2.1–8, 11–14 Psalm 34.1–6 or 37.3–5, 30–32 Luke 17.7–10	Psalms **21**, 24 or **73** Isaiah 5.25–end Matthew 5.13–20	Psalms 36, **40** or **74** Daniel 5.1–12 Revelation 6
Wednesday	**13 November** *Rw/Gw* Charles Simeon, priest, evangelical divine, 1836 (see p.80)	Wisdom 6.1–11 or Titus 3.1–7 Psalm 82 or 23 Luke 17.11–19	Psalms **23**, 25 or **77** Isaiah 6 Matthew 5.21–37	Psalm **37** or **119.81–104** Daniel 5.13–end Revelation 7.1–4, 9–end
Thursday	**14 November** *R/G* Samuel Seabury, bishop, 1796	Wisdom 7.22—8.1 or Philemon vv 7–20 Psalm 119.89–96 or 146.4–end Luke 17.20–25	Psalms **26**, 27 or **78.1–39*** Isaiah 7.1–17 Matthew 5.38–end	Psalms 42, **43** or **78.40–end*** Daniel 6 Revelation 8
Friday	**15 November** *R/G*	Wisdom 13.1–9 or 2 John 4–9 Psalm 19.1–4 or 119.1–8 Luke 17.26–end	Psalms 28, **32** or **55** Isaiah 8.1–15 Matthew 6.1–18	Psalm 31 or **69** Daniel 7.1–14 Revelation 9.1–12
Saturday	**16 November** *Rw/Gw* Margaret, queen, philanthropist, 1093 (see p.82) *Edmund Rich, archbishop, 1240*	Wisdom 18.14–16, 19.6–9 or 3 John 5–8 Psalm 105.1–5, 35–42 or 112 Luke 18.1–8	Psalm 33 or **76**, 79 Isaiah 8.16—9.7 Matthew 6.19–end	Psalms 84, **86** or 81, **84** Daniel 7.15–end Revelation 9.13–end

		Principal Service	3rd Service	2nd Service
Sunday	**17 November** *R/G* **2nd Sunday before Advent**	Malachi 4.1–2a Psalm 98 2 Thessalonians 3.6–13 Luke 21.5–19	Psalm 132 1 Samuel 16.1–13 Matthew 13.44–52	Psalms [93] 97 Daniel 6 Matthew 13.1–9, 18–23
		Holy Communion	**Morning Prayer**	**Evening Prayer**
Monday	**18 November** *Rw/Gw* Elizabeth, princess, philanthropist, 1231 (see p.82) DEL week 33	1 Maccabees 1.10–15, 41–43, 54–57, 62–64 or Revelation 1.1–4, 2.1–5 Psalm 79.1–5 or 1 Luke 18.35–end	Psalms 46, **47** or 80, **82** Isaiah 9.8–10.4 Matthew 7.1–12	Psalms 70, **71** or **85**, 86 Daniel 8.1–14 Revelation 10
Tuesday	**19 November** *Rw/Gw* Hilda, abbess, 680 (see p.81) *Mechtild, béguine, mystic, 1280*	2 Maccabees 6.18–end or Revelation 3.1–6, 14–31 Psalm 11 or 15 *Luke 19.1–10*	Psalms 48, **52** or 87, **89.1–18** Isaiah 10.5–19 Matthew 7.13–end	Psalms **67**, 72 or **89.19–end** Daniel 8.15–end Revelation 11.1–14
Wednesday	**20 November** *R/Gr* Edmund, king, martyr, 870 (see p.78) *Priscilla Lydia Sellon, a restorer of the* *religious life in the Church of England, 1876*	2 Maccabees 7.1, 20–31 or Revelation 4 Psalm 116.10–end or 150 Luke 19.11–28	Psalms **56**, 57 or 119.**105–128** Isaiah 10.20–32 Matthew 8.1–13	Psalm **73** or **91**, 93 Daniel 9.1–19 Revelation 11.15–end
Thursday	**21 November** *R/G*	1 Maccabees 2.15–29 or Revelation 5.1–10 Psalm 129 or 149.1–5 Luke 19.41–44	Psalms 61, **62** or 90, **92** Isaiah 10.33—11.9 Matthew 8.14–22	Psalms 74, **76** or **94** Daniel 9.20–end Revelation 12
Friday	**22 November** *R/G* *Cecilia, martyr, c.230*	1 Maccabees 4.36–37, 52–59 or Revelation 10.8–11 Psalm 122 or 119.65–72 Luke 19.45–48	Psalms **63**, 65 or 88 (95) Isaiah 11.10—end of 12 Matthew 8.23–end	Psalm **77** or 102 Daniel 10.1—11.1 Revelation 13.1–10
Saturday	**23 November** *R/Gr* Clement, bishop, martyr, c.100 (see p.78)	1 Maccabees 6.1–13 or Revelation 11.4–12 Psalm 124 or 144.1–9 Luke 20.27–40	Psalm **78.1–39** or 96, **97**, 100 Isaiah 13.1–13 Matthew 9.1–17	Psalm **78.40–end** or 104 Daniel 12 Revelation 13.11–end or: 1st EP of Christ the King: Psalms 99, 100; Isaiah 10.33—11.9; 1 Timothy 6.11–16

Christ the King / Sunday next before Advent

		Principal Service	3rd Service	2nd Service
		Holy Communion	**Morning Prayer**	**Evening Prayer**
Sunday	**24 November** R/W — Christ the King — Sunday next before Advent	Jeremiah 23.1–6 / Psalm 46 / Colossians 1.11–20 / Luke 23.33–43	MP Psalms 29, 110 / Zechariah 6.9–end / Revelation 11.15–18	EP Psalm 72 [or 72.1–7] / 1 Samuel 8.4–end / John 18.33–37
Monday	**25 November** R/G — Catherine, martyr, 4th cent. — Isaac Watts, hymn writer, 1748 — DEL week 34	Daniel 1.1–6, 8–20 / Canticle: Bless the Lord / Luke 21.1–4	Psalms 92, 96 or 98, 99, 101 / Isaiah 14.3–20 / Matthew 9.18–34	Psalms 80, 81 or **105*** (or 103) / Isaiah 40.1–11 / Revelation 14.1–13
Tuesday	**26 November** R/G	Daniel 2.31–45 / Canticle: Benedicite vv 1–3 / Luke 21.5–11	Psalms **97**, 98, 100 or **106*** (or 103) / Isaiah 17 / Matthew 9.35—10.15	Psalms 99, **101** or **107*** / Isaiah 40.12–26 / Revelation 14.14—end of 15
Wednesday	**27 November** R/G	Daniel 5.1–6, 13–14, 16–17, 23–28 / Canticle: Benedicite vv 4–5 / Luke 21.12–19	Psalms 110, 111, **112** or 110, **111**, 112 / Isaiah 19 / Matthew 10.16–33	Psalms 121, **122**, 123, 124 or **119.129–152** / Isaiah 40.27—41.7 / Revelation 16.1–11
Thursday	**28 November** R/G	Daniel 6.12–end / Canticle: Benedicite vv 6–8a / Luke 21.20–28	Psalms **125**, 126, 127, 128 or 113, **115** / Isaiah 21.1–12 / Matthew 10.34—11.1	Psalms 131, 132, **133** or 114, **116**, 117 / Isaiah 41.8–20 / Revelation 16.12–end
Friday	**29 November** R/G — Day of Intercession and Thanksgiving for the Missionary Work of the Church	Daniel 7.2–14 / Canticle: Benedicite vv 8b–10a / Luke 21.29–33	Psalm **139** / Isaiah 22.1–14 / Matthew 11.2–19	Psalms **146**, 147 or **130**, 131, 137 / Isaiah 41.21—42.9 / Revelation 17 / or: 1st EP of Andrew the Apostle: Psalm 48; Isaiah 49.1–9a; 1 Corinthians 4.9–16
		Principal Service	**3rd Service**	**2nd Service**
Saturday	**30 November** R — Andrew the Apostle	Isaiah 52.7–10 / Psalm 19.1–6 / Romans 10.12–18 / Matthew 4.18–22	MP Psalms 47, 147.1–12 / Ezekiel 47.1–12 or Ecclesiasticus 14.20–end / John 12.20–32	EP Psalms 87, 96 / Zechariah 8.20–end / John 1.35–42

66

¶ *Additional Weekday Lectionary*

This Additional Weekday Lectionary provides two readings for each day of the year, except for Sundays, Principal Feasts and other Principal Holy Days, Holy Week and Festivals (for which the readings provided in the main body of this lectionary are used). The readings for 'first evensongs' in the main body of the lectionary are used on the eves of Principal Feasts and may be used on the eves of Festivals. This lectionary is intended particularly for use in those places of worship that attract occasional rather than daily worshippers, and can be used either at Morning or Evening Prayer. Psalmody is not provided and should be taken from the daily provision earlier in this volume.

		2 December – Advent 1	
Monday	3 December	Malachi 3.1–6	Matthew 3.1–6
Tuesday	4 December	Zephaniah 3.14–end	1 Thessalonians 4.13–end
Wednesday	5 December	Isaiah 65.17—66.2	Matthew 24.1–14
Thursday	6 December	Micah 5.2–5*a*	John 3.16–21
Friday	7 December	Isaiah 66.18–end	Luke 13.22–30
Saturday	8 December	Micah 7.8–15	Romans 15.30—16.7, 25–end
		9 December – Advent 2	
Monday	10 December	Jeremiah 7.1–11	Philippians 4.4–9
Tuesday	11 December	Daniel 7.9–14	Matthew 24.15–28
Wednesday	12 December	Amos 9.11–end	Romans 13.8–14
Thursday	13 December	Jeremiah 23.5–8	Mark 11.1–11
Friday	14 December	Jeremiah 33.14–22	Luke 21.25–36
Saturday	15 December	Zechariah 14.4–11	Revelation 22.1–7
		16 December – Advent 3	
Monday	17 December	Ecclesiasticus 24.1–9 or Proverbs 8.22–31	1 Corinthians 2.1–13
Tuesday	18 December	Exodus 3.1–6	Acts 7.20–36
Wednesday	19 December	Isaiah 11.1–9	Romans 15.7–13
Thursday	20 December	Isaiah 22.21–23	Revelation 3.7–13
Friday	21 December	Numbers 24.15*b*–19	Revelation 22.10–21
Saturday	22 December	Jeremiah 30.7–11*a*	Acts 4.1–12
		23 December – Advent 4	
Monday	24 December	At Evening Prayer the readings for **Christmas Eve** are used (see page 13). At other services, the following readings are used:	
		Isaiah 29.13–18	1 John 4.7–16
Tuesday	25 December	Christmas Day – see p.13	
Wednesday	26 December	Stephen, deacon, martyr – see p.13	
Thursday	27 December	John, Apostle and Evangelist – see p.13	
Friday	28 December	The Holy Innocents – see p.13	
Saturday	29 December	Micah 1.1–4; 2.12–13	Luke 2.1–7
		30 December – Christmas 1	
Monday	31 December	Ecclesiastes 3.1–13 or 1st EP of the Naming and Circumcision of Jesus	Revelation 21.1–8
Tuesday	1 January	Naming and Circumcision of Jesus– see p.14	
Wednesday	2 January	Isaiah 66.6–14	Matthew 12.46–50
Thursday	3 January	Deuteronomy 6.4–15	John 10.31–end
Friday	4 January	Isaiah 63.7–16	Galatians 3.23—4.7
Saturday	5 January	At Evening Prayer the readings for the Eve of Epiphany (see p. 14) are used. At other services, the following readings are used:	
		Isaiah 12	2 Corinthians 2.12–end

Monday	7 January	Genesis 25.19–end	Ephesians 1.1–6
Tuesday	8 January	Joel 2.28–end	Ephesians 1.7–14
Wednesday	9 January	Proverbs 8.12–21	Ephesians 1.15–end
Thursday	10 January	Genesis 19.15–29	Ephesians 2.1–10
Friday	11 January	Genesis 17.1–14	Ephesians 2.11–end
Saturday	12 January	1 Kings 10.1–13	Ephesians 3.14–end
		or 1st EP of the Baptism of Christ	

Monday	14 January	Isaiah 41.14–20	John 1.29–34
Tuesday	15 January	Exodus 17.1–7	Acts 8.26–end
Wednesday	16 January	Exodus 15.1–19	Colossians 2.8–15
Thursday	17 January	Zechariah 6.9–15	1 Peter 2.4–10
Friday	18 January	Isaiah 51.7–16	Galatians 6.14–18
Saturday	19 January	Leviticus 16.11–22	Hebrews 10.19–25

Monday	21 January	1 Kings 17.8–16	Mark 8.1–10
Tuesday	22 January	1 Kings 19.1–9a	Mark 1.9–15
Wednesday	23 January	1 Kings 19.9b–18	Mark 9.2–13
Thursday	24 January	Leviticus 11.1–8, 13–19, 41–45	Acts 10.9–16
		or 1st EP of the Conversion of Paul	
Friday	25 January	Conversion of Paul – see p.17	
Saturday	26 January	Genesis 35.1–15	Acts 10.44–end

Monday	28 January	Ezekiel 37.15–end	John 17.1–19
Tuesday	29 January	Ezekiel 20.39–44	John 17.20–end
Wednesday	30 January	Nehemiah 2.1–10	Romans 12.1–8
Thursday	31 January	Deuteronomy 26.16–end	Romans 14.1–9
Friday	1 February	Leviticus 19.9–28	Romans 15.1–7
		or 1st EP of the Presentation of Christ	
Saturday	2 February	Presentation of Christ in the Temple – see p.18	
		or, if the Presentation *is celebrated on Sunday 3 February,*	
		Jeremiah 33.1–11; 1 Peter 5.5b–end	
		or 1st EP of Presentation of Christ – see p.18	

Monday	4 February	Isaiah 61.1–9	Mark 6.1–13
Tuesday	5 February	Isaiah 52.1–10	Romans 10.5–21
Wednesday	6 February	Isaiah 52.13—53.6	Romans 15.14–21
Thursday	7 February	Isaiah 53.4–12	2 Corinthians 4.1–10
Friday	8 February	Zechariah 8.16–end	Matthew 10.1–15
Saturday	9 February	Jeremiah 1.4–10	Matthew 10.16–22

Monday	11 February	2 Kings 2.13–22	3 John
Tuesday	12 February	Judges 14.5–17	Revelation 10.4–11
Wednesday	13 February	Ash Wednesday – see p.20	
Thursday	14 February	Genesis 2.7–end	Hebrews 2.5–end
Friday	15 February	Genesis 4.1–12	Hebrews 4.12–end
Saturday	16 February	2 Kings 22.11–end	Hebrews 5.1–10

Monday	18 February	Genesis 6.11–end, 7.11–16	Luke 4.14–21
Tuesday	19 February	Deuteronomy 31.7–13	1 John 3.1–10
Wednesday	20 February	Genesis 11.1–9	Matthew 24.15–28
Thursday	21 February	Genesis 13.1–13	1 Peter 2.13–end
Friday	22 February	Genesis 21.1–8	Luke 9.18–27
Saturday	23 February	Genesis 32.22–32	2 Peter 1.10–end

Monday	25 February	I Chronicles 21.1–17	I John 2.1–8
Tuesday	26 February	Zechariah 3	2 Peter 2.1–10a
Wednesday	27 February	Job 1.1–22	Luke 21.34—22.6
Thursday	28 February	2 Chronicles 29.1–11	Mark 11.15–19
Friday	I March	Exodus 19.1–9a	I Peter 1.1–9
Saturday	2 March	Exodus 19.9b–19	Acts 7.44–50

3 March – Lent 3

Monday	4 March	Joshua 4.1–13	Luke 9.1–11
Tuesday	5 March	Exodus 15.22–27	Hebrews 10.32–end
Wednesday	6 March	Genesis 9.8–17	I Peter 3.18–end
Thursday	7 March	Daniel 12.5–end	Mark 13.21–end
Friday	8 March	Numbers 20.1–13	I Corinthians 10.23–end
Saturday	9 March	Isaiah 43.14–end	Hebrews 3.1–15

10 March – Lent 4

Monday	11 March	2 Kings 24.18—25.7	I Corinthians 15.20–34
Tuesday	12 March	Jeremiah 13.12–19	Acts 13.26–35
Wednesday	13 March	Jeremiah 13.20–27	I Peter 1.17—2.3
Thursday	14 March	Jeremiah 22.11–19	Luke 11.37–52
Friday	15 March	Jeremiah 17.1–14	Luke 6.17–26
Saturday	16 March	Ezra I	2 Corinthians 1.12–19

17 March – Lent 5

Monday	18 March	Joel 2.12–17	2 John
		or 1st EP of Joseph of Nazareth	
Tuesday	19 March	Joseph of Nazareth – see p.25	
Wednesday	20 March	Job 36.1–12	John 14.1–14
Thursday	21 March	Jeremiah 9.17–22	Luke 13.31–35
Friday	22 March	Lamentations 5.1–3, 19–22	John 12.20–26
Saturday	23 March	Job 17.6–end	John 12.27–36

24 March – Palm Sunday

From the Monday of Holy Week until Easter Eve the seasonal lectionary is used: see pp.26–27.

31 March – Easter

Monday	I April	Isaiah 54.1–14	Romans 1.1–7
Tuesday	2 April	Isaiah 51.1–11	John 5.19–29
Wednesday	3 April	Isaiah 26.1–19	John 20.1–10
Thursday	4 April	Isaiah 43.14–21	Revelation 1.4–end
Friday	5 April	Isaiah 42.10–17	I Thessalonians 5.1–11
Saturday	6 April	Job 14.1–14	John 21.1–14

7 April – Easter 2

Monday	8 April	Annunciation of Our Lord to the Blessed Virgin Mary – see p.29	
Tuesday	9 April	Proverbs 8.1–11	Acts 16.6–15
Wednesday	10 April	Hosea 5.15—6.6	I Corinthians 15.1–11
Thursday	11 April	Jonah 2	Mark 4.35–end
Friday	12 April	Genesis 6.9–end	I Peter 3.8–end
Saturday	13 April	I Samuel 2.1–8	Matthew 28.8–15

14 April – Easter 3

Monday	15 April	Exodus 24.1–11	Revelation 5
Tuesday	16 April	Leviticus 19.9–18, 32–end	Matthew 5.38–end
Wednesday	17 April	Genesis 3.8–21	I Corinthians 15.12–28
Thursday	18 April	Isaiah 33.13–22	Mark 6.47–end
Friday	19 April	Nehemiah 9.6–17	Romans 5.12–end
Saturday	20 April	Isaiah 61.10—62.5	Luke 24.1–12

Monday	**22 April**	Jeremiah 31.10–17	Revelation 7.9–end
		or 1st EP of George, martyr, patron of England	
Tuesday	**23 April**	George, martyr, patron of England – see p.31	
Wednesday	**24 April**	Genesis 2.4b–9	1 Corinthians 15.35–49
		or 1st EP of Mark the Evangelist	
Thursday	**25 April**	Mark the Evangelist – see p.31	
Friday	**26 April**	Ecclesiastes 12.1–8	Romans 6.1–11
Saturday	**27 April**	1 Chronicles 29.10–13	Luke 24.13–35

Monday	**29 April**	Genesis 15.1–18	Romans 4.13–end
Tuesday	**30 April**	Deuteronomy 8.1–10	Matthew 6.19–end
		or 1st EP of Philip and James, Apostles	
Wednesday	**1 May**	Philip and James, Apostles – see p.32	
Thursday	**2 May**	Exodus 3.1–15	Mark 12.18–27
Friday	**3 May**	Ezekiel 36.33–end	Romans 8.1–11
Saturday	**4 May**	Isaiah 38.9–20	Luke 24.33–end

Monday	**6 May**	Proverbs 4.1–13	Philippians 2.1–11
Tuesday	**7 May**	Isaiah 32.12–end	Romans 5.1–11
Wednesday	**8 May**	*At Evening Prayer the readings for the Eve of Ascension Day are used. At other services, the following readings are used:*	
		Isaiah 43.1–13	Titus 2.11—3.8
Thursday	**9 May**	Ascension Day – see p.33	
Friday	**10 May**	Exodus 35.30—36.1	Galatians 5.13–end
Saturday	**11 May**	Numbers 11.16–17, 24–29	1 Corinthians 2

Monday	**13 May**	Numbers 27.15–end	1 Corinthians 3
		or 1st EP of Matthias the Apostle	
Tuesday	**14 May**	Matthias the Apostle – see p.35	
		If Matthias the Apostle *is celebrated on 25 February, the following readings are used:*	
		1 Samuel 10.1–10	1 Corinthians 12.1–13
Wednesday	**15 May**	1 Kings 19.1–18	Matthew 3.13–end
Thursday	**16 May**	Ezekiel 11.14–20	Matthew 9.35—10.20
Friday	**17 May**	Ezekiel 36.22–28	Matthew 12.22–32
Saturday	**18 May**	*At Evening Prayer the readings for the Eve of Pentecost are used. At other services, the following readings are used:*	
		Micah 3.1–8	Ephesians 6.10–20

Monday	**20 May**	Genesis 12.1–9	Romans 4.13–end
Tuesday	**21 May**	Genesis 13.1–12	Romans 12.9–end
Wednesday	**22 May**	Genesis 15	Romans 4.1–8
Thursday	**23 May**	Genesis 22.1–18	Hebrews 11.8–19
Friday	**24 May**	Isaiah 51.1–8	John 8.48–end
Saturday	**25 May**	*At Evening Prayer the readings for the Eve of Trinity Sunday are used. At other services, the following readings are used:*	
		Ecclesiasticus 44.19–23	James 2.14–26
		or Joshua 2.1–15	

Monday	**27 May**	Exodus 2.1–10	Hebrews 11.23–31
Tuesday	**28 May**	Exodus 2.11–end	Acts 7.17–29
Wednesday	**29 May**	Exodus 3.1–12	Acts 7.30–38
		or 1st EP of Corpus Christi	
Thursday	**30 May**	Day of Thanksgiving for the Institution of the Holy Communion (Corpus Christi) – see p.38	
		or, where Corpus Christi *is celebrated as a Lesser Festival:*	
		Exodus 6.1–13	John 9.24–38
		or 1st EP of Visit of the Blessed Virgin Mary to Elizabeth	
Friday	**31 May**	Visit of the Blessed Virgin Mary to Elizabeth – see p.38	
Saturday	**1 June**	Exodus 34.27–end	2 Corinthians 3.7–end

Monday	**3 June**	Genesis 37.1–11	Romans 11.9–21
Tuesday	**4 June**	Genesis 41.15–40	Mark 13.1–13
Wednesday	**5 June**	Genesis 42.17–end	Matthew 18.1–14
Thursday	**6 June**	Genesis 45.1–15	Acts 7.9–16
Friday	**7 June**	Genesis 47.1–12	1 Thessalonians 5.12–end
Saturday	**8 June**	Genesis 50.4–21	Luke 15.11–end

Monday	**10 June**	Isaiah 32	James 3.13–end
Tuesday	**11 June**	Proverbs 3.1–18	Matthew 5.1–12
		or 1st EP of Barnabas	
		Barnabas the Apostle – see p.40	
Wednesday	**12 June**	Judges 6.1–16	Matthew 5.13–24
Thursday	**13 June**	Jeremiah 6.9–15	1 Timothy 2.1–6
Friday	**14 June**	1 Samuel 16.14–end	John 14.15–end
Saturday	**15 June**	Isaiah 6.1–9	Revelation 19.9–end

Monday	**17 June**	Exodus 13.13b–end	Luke 15.1–10
Tuesday	**18 June**	Proverbs 1.20–end	James 5.13–end
Wednesday	**19 June**	Isaiah 5.8–24	James 1.17–25
Thursday	**20 June**	Isaiah 57.14–end	John 13.1–17
Friday	**21 June**	Jeremiah 15.15–end	Luke 16.19–31
Saturday	**22 June**	Isaiah 25.1–9	Acts 2.22–33

Monday	**24 June**	Birth of John the Baptist – see p.42	
Tuesday	**25 June**	Proverbs 6.6–19	Luke 4.1–14
Wednesday	**26 June**	Isaiah 24.1–15	1 Corinthians 6.1–11
Thursday	**27 June**	Job 7	Matthew 7.21–29
Friday	**28 June**	Jeremiah 20.7–end	Matthew 27.27–44
		or 1st EP of Peter and Paul, Apostles	
Saturday	**29 June**	Peter and Paul, Apostles (*or* Peter the Apostle) – see p.42	

Monday	**1 July**	Exodus 32.1–14	Colossians 3.1–11
Tuesday	**2 July**	Proverbs 9.1–12	2 Thessalonians 2.13—3.5
		or 1st EP of Thomas the Apostle	
Wednesday	**3 July**	Thomas the Apostle – see p.43	
		If Thomas the Apostle *is celebrated on 21 December, the following readings are used:*	
		Isaiah 26.1–9	Romans 8.12–27
Thursday	**4 July**	Jeremiah 8.18—9.6	John 13.21–35
Friday	**5 July**	2 Samuel 5.1–12	Matthew 27.45–56
Saturday	**6 July**	Hosea 11.1–11	Matthew 28.1–7

Monday	8 July	Exodus 40.1–16	Luke 14.15–24
Tuesday	9 July	Proverbs 11.1–12	Mark 12.38–44
Wednesday	10 July	Isaiah 33.2–10	Philippians 1.1–11
Thursday	11 July	Job 38	Luke 18.1–14
Friday	12 July	Job 42.1–6	John 3.1–15
Saturday	13 July	Ecclesiastes 9.1–11	Hebrews 1.1–9

Monday	15 July	Numbers 23.1–12	1 Corinthians 1.10–17
Tuesday	16 July	Proverbs 12.1–12	Galatians 3.1–14
Wednesday	17 July	Isaiah 49.8–13	2 Corinthians 8.1–11
Thursday	18 July	Hosea 14	John 15.1–17
Friday	19 July	2 Samuel 18.18–end	Matthew 27.57–66
Saturday	20 July	Isaiah 55.1–7	Mark 16.1–8

Monday	22 July	Mary Magdalene – see p.46	
Tuesday	23 July	Proverbs 12.13–end	John 1.43–51
Wednesday	24 July	Isaiah 55.8–end	2 Timothy 2.8–19
		or 1st EP of James the Apostle	
Thursday	25 July	James the Apostle – see p.46	
Friday	26 July	Jeremiah 14.1–9	Luke 8.4–15
Saturday	27 July	Ecclesiastes 5.10–19	1 Timothy 6.6–16

Monday	29 July	Joshua 1.1–9	1 Corinthians 9.19–end
Tuesday	30 July	Proverbs 15.1–11	Galatians 2.15–end
Wednesday	31 July	Isaiah 49.1–7	1 John 1
Thursday	1 August	Proverbs 27.1–12	John 15.12–27
Friday	2 August	Isaiah 59.8–end	Mark 15.6–20
Saturday	3 August	Zechariah 7.8—8.8	Luke 20.27–40

Monday	5 August	Judges 13.1–23	Luke 10.38–42
		or 1st EP of the Transfiguration of Our Lord	
Tuesday	6 August	Transfiguration of Our Lord – see p.48	
Wednesday	7 August	Isaiah 45.1–7	Ephesians 4.1–16
Thursday	8 August	Jeremiah 16.1–15	Luke 12.35–48
Friday	9 August	Jeremiah 18.1–11	Hebrews 1.1–9
Saturday	10 August	Jeremiah 26.1–19	Ephesians 3.1–13

Monday	12 August	Ruth 2.1–13	Luke 10.25–37
Tuesday	13 August	Proverbs 16.1–11	Philippians 3.4b–end
Wednesday	14 August	Deuteronomy 11.1–21	2 Corinthians 9.6–end
		or 1st EP of The Blessed Virgin Mary	
Thursday	15 August	The Blessed Virgin Mary – see p.49	
		If The Blessed Virgin Mary is celebrated on 8 or 9 September, the following readings are used:	
		Ecclesiasticus 2	John 16.1–15
		or Ecclesiastes 2.12–25	
Friday	16 August	Obadiah vv 1–10	John 19.1–16
Saturday	17 August	2 Kings 2.11–14	Luke 24.36–end

Monday	19 August	1 Samuel 17.32–50	Matthew 8.14–22
Tuesday	20 August	Proverbs 17.1–15	Luke 7.1–17
Wednesday	21 August	Jeremiah 5.20–end	2 Peter 3.8–end
Thursday	22 August	Daniel 2.1–23	Luke 10.1–20
Friday	23 August	Daniel 3.1–28	Revelation 15
		or 1st EP of Bartholomew the Apostle	
Saturday	24 August	Bartholomew the Apostle – see p.50	

Monday	26 August	2 Samuel 7.4–17	2 Corinthians 5.1–10
Tuesday	27 August	Proverbs 18.10–21	Romans 14.10–end
Wednesday	28 August	Judges 4.1–10	Romans 1.8–17
Thursday	29 August	Isaiah 49.14–end	John 16.16–24
Friday	30 August	Job 9.1–24	Mark 15.21–32
Saturday	31 August	Exodus 19.1–9	John 20.11–18

Monday	2 September	Haggai 1	Mark 7.9–23
Tuesday	3 September	Proverbs 21.1–18	Mark 6.30–44
Wednesday	4 September	Hosea 11.1–11	1 John 4.9–end
Thursday	5 September	Lamentations 3.34–48	Romans 7.14–end
Friday	6 September	2 Kings 19.4–18	1 Thessalonians 3
Saturday	7 September	Ecclesiasticus 4.11–28	2 Timothy 3.10–end
		or Deuteronomy 29.2–15	

Monday	9 September	Wisdom 6.12–21	Matthew 15.1–9
		or Job 12.1–16	
Tuesday	10 September	Proverbs 8.1–11	Luke 6.39–end
Wednesday	11 September	Proverbs 2.1–15	Colossians 1.9–20
Thursday	12 September	Baruch 3.14–end	John 1.1–18
		or Genesis 1.1–13	
Friday	13 September	Ecclesiasticus 1.1–20	1 Corinthians 1.18–end
		or Deuteronomy 7.7–16	
		or 1st EP of Holy Cross Day	
Saturday	14 September	Holy Cross Day – see p.53	

Monday	16 September	Genesis 21.1–13	Luke 1.26–38
Tuesday	17 September	Ruth 4.7–17	Luke 2.25–38
Wednesday	18 September	2 Kings 4.1–7	John 2.1–11
Thursday	19 September	2 Kings 4.25b–37	Mark 3.19b–35
Friday	20 September	Judith 8.9–17, 28–36	John 19.25b–30
		or Ruth 1.1–18	
		or 1st EP of Matthew, Apostle and Evangelist	
Saturday	21 September	Matthew, Apostle and Evangelist – see p.54	

Monday	23 September	Exodus 19.16–end	Hebrews 12.18–end
Tuesday	24 September	1 Chronicles 16.1–13	Revelation 11.15–end
Wednesday	25 September	1 Chronicles 29.10–19	Colossians 3.12–17
Thursday	26 September	Nehemiah 8.1–12	1 Corinthians 14.1–12
Friday	27 September	Isaiah 1.10–17	Mark 12.28–34
Saturday	28 September	Daniel 6.6–23	Revelation 12.7–12
		or 1st EP of Michael and All Angels	

Monday	30 September	2 Samuel 22.4–7, 17–20	Hebrews 7.26—8.6
		or Michael and All Angels transferred – see p.56	
Tuesday	1 October	Proverbs 22.17–end	2 Corinthians 12.1–10
Wednesday	2 October	Hosea 14	James 2.14–26
Thursday	3 October	Isaiah 24.1–15	John 16.25–33
Friday	4 October	Jeremiah 14.1–9	Luke 23.44–56
Saturday	5 October	Zechariah 8.14–end	John 20.19–end

Monday	7 October	1 Kings 3.3–14	1 Timothy 3.14—4.8
Tuesday	8 October	Proverbs 27.11–end	Galatians 6.1–10
Wednesday	9 October	Isaiah 51.1–6	2 Corinthians 1.1–11
Thursday	10 October	Ecclesiasticus 18.1–14	1 Corinthians 11.17–end
		or Job 26	
Friday	11 October	Ecclesiasticus 28.2–12	Mark 15.33–47
		or Job 19.21–end	
Saturday	12 October	Isaiah 44.21–end	John 21.15–end

Monday	14 October	1 Kings 6.2–10	John 12.1–11
Tuesday	15 October	Proverbs 31.10–end	Luke 10.38–42
Wednesday	16 October	Jonah 1	Luke 5.1–11
Thursday	17 October	Exodus 12.1–20	1 Thessalonians 4.1–12
		or 1st EP of Luke the Evangelist	
Friday	18 October	Luke the Evangelist – see p.59	
Saturday	19 October	2 Samuel 7.18–end	Acts 2.22–33

Monday	21 October	1 Kings 8.22–30	John 12.12–19
Tuesday	22 October	Ecclesiastes 11	Luke 13.10–17
Wednesday	23 October	Hosea 14.1–7	2 Timothy 4.1–8
Thursday	24 October	Isaiah 49.1–7	John 19.16–25a
Friday	25 October	Proverbs 24.3–22	John 8.1–11
Saturday	26 October	Ecclesiasticus 7.8–17, 32–end	2 Timothy 1.1–14
		or Deuteronomy 6.16–25	

Monday	28 October	Simon and Jude, Apostles – see p.61	
Tuesday	29 October	1 Samuel 4.12–end	Luke 1.57–80
Wednesday	30 October	Baruch 5	Mark 1.1–11
		or Haggai 1.1–11	
Thursday	31 October	Isaiah 35	Matthew 11.2–19
		or 1st EP of All Saints' Day	
Friday	1 November	All Saints' Day – see p.62	
		or, if All Saints' Day *is celebrated on Sunday 3 November only:*	
		2 Samuel 11.1–17	Matthew 14.1–12
Saturday	2 November	Isaiah 43.15–21	Acts 19.1–10
		or, if All Saints' Day *is celebrated on Sunday 3 November only,*	
		1st EP of All Saints' Day	

Monday	4 November	Esther 3.1–11, 4.7–17	Matthew 18.1–10
Tuesday	5 November	Ezekiel 18.21–end	Matthew 18.12–20
Wednesday	6 November	Proverbs 3.27–end	Matthew 18.21–end
Thursday	7 November	Exodus 23.1–9	Matthew 19.1–15
Friday	8 November	Proverbs 3.13–18	Matthew 19.16–end
Saturday	9 November	Deuteronomy 28.1–6	Matthew 20.1–16

Monday	**11 November**	Isaiah 40.21–end	Romans 11.25–end
Tuesday	**12 November**	Ezekiel 34.20–end	John 10.1–18
Wednesday	**13 November**	Leviticus 26.3–13	Titus 2.1–10
Thursday	**14 November**	Hosea 6.1–6	Matthew 9.9–13
Friday	**15 November**	Malachi 4	John 4.5–26
Saturday	**16 November**	Micah 6.6–8	Colossians 3.12–17

17 November – 2 before Advent

Monday	**18 November**	Micah 7.1–7	Matthew 10.24–39
Tuesday	**19 November**	Habakkuk 3.1–19a	1 Corinthians 4.9–16
Wednesday	**20 November**	Zechariah 8.1–13	Mark 13.3–8
Thursday	**21 November**	Zechariah 10.6–end	1 Peter 5.1–11
Friday	**22 November**	Micah 4.1–5	Luke 9.28–36
Saturday	**23 November**	*At Evening Prayer the readings for the Eve of Christ the King are used. At other services, the following readings are used:*	
		Exodus 16.1–21	John 6.3–15

24 November – Christ the King (Sunday next before Advent)

Monday	**25 November**	Jeremiah 30.1–3, 10–17	Romans 12.9–21
Tuesday	**26 November**	Jeremiah 30.18–24	John 10.22–30
Wednesday	**27 November**	Jeremiah 31.1–9	Matthew 15.21–31
Thursday	**28 November**	Jeremiah 31.10–17	Matthew 16.13–end
Friday	**29 November**	Jeremiah 31.31–37	Hebrews 10.11–18
		or 1st EP of Andrew the Apostle	
Saturday	**30 November**	Andrew the Apostle – see p.66	

¶ Collects and Post Communions

All the contemporary language Collects and Post Communions, including the Additional Collects, may be found in *Common Worship: Collects and Post Communions* (Church House Publishing: London, 2004). The Additional Collects are also published separately.

The contemporary language Collects and Post Communions all appear in *Times and Seasons: President's Edition for Holy Communion*. Apart from the Additional Collects, they appear in the other Common Worship volumes as follows:

¶ President's edition: all Collects and Post Communions;
¶ *Daily Prayer*: all Collects;
¶ main volume: Collects and Post Communions for Sundays, Principal Feasts and Holy Days, and Festivals;
¶ *Festivals*: Collects and Post Communions for Festivals, Lesser Festivals, Common of the Saints and Special Occasions.

The traditional-language Collects and Post Communions all appear in the president's edition. They appear in other publications as follows:

¶ main volume: Collects and Post Communions for Sundays, Principal Feasts and Holy Days, and Festivals;
¶ separate booklet: Collects and Post Communions for Lesser Festivals, Common of the Saints and Special Occasions.

¶ Lectionary for Dedication Festival

If date not known, observe on the first Sunday in October or Last Sunday after Trinity.

Evening Prayer on the Eve	Psalm 24 2 Chronicles 7.11–16 John 4.19–29

Dedication Festival   *Gold or White*

	Principal Service	3rd Service	2nd Service	Psalmody
Year A	1 Kings 8.22–30 or Revelation 21.9–14 Psalm 122 Hebrews 12.18–24 Matthew 21.12–16	Haggai 2.6–9 Hebrews 10.19–25	Jeremiah 7.1–11 1 Corinthians 3.9–17 *HC* Luke 19.1–10	*MP* 48, 150 *EP* 132
Year B	Genesis 28.11–18 or Revelation 21.9–14 Psalm 122 1 Peter 2.1–10 John 10.22–29	Haggai 2.6–9 Hebrews 10.19–25	Jeremiah 7.1–11 Luke 19.1–10	*MP* 48, 150 *EP* 132
Year C	1 Chronicles 29.6–19 Psalm 122 Ephesians 2.19–22 John 2.13–22	Haggai 2.6–9 Hebrews 10.19–25	Jeremiah 7.1–11 Luke 19.1–10	*MP* 48, 150 *EP* 132

The Blessed Virgin Mary

Genesis 3.8–15, 20; Isaiah 7.10–14; Micah 5.1–4
Psalms 45.10–17; 113; 131
Acts 1.12–14; Romans 8.18–30; Galatians 4.4–7
Luke 1.26–38; *or* 1.39–47; John 19.25–27

Martyrs

2 Chronicles 24.17–21; Isaiah 43.1–7; Jeremiah 11.18–20; Wisdom 4.10–15
Psalms 3; 11; 31.1–5; 44.18–24; 126
Romans 8.35–end; 2 Corinthians 4.7–15; 2 Timothy 2.3–7 [8–13]; Hebrews 11.32–end;
    1 Peter 4.12–end; Revelation 12.10–12a
Matthew 10.16–22; *or* 10.28–39; *or* 16.24–26; John 12.24–26; *or* 15.18–21

Agnes (21 Jan): *also* Revelation 7.13–end
Alban (22 June): *especially* 2 Timothy 2.3–13; John 12.24–26
Alphege (19 Apr): *also* Hebrews 5.1–4
Boniface (5 June): *also* Acts 20.24–28
Charles (30 Jan): *also* Ecclesiasticus 2.12–end; 1 Timothy 6.12–16
Clement (23 Nov): *also* Philippians 3.17—4.3; Matthew 16.13–19
Cyprian (15 Sept): *especially* 1 Peter 4.12–end; *also* Matthew 18.18–22
Edmund (20 Nov): *also* Proverbs 20.28; 21.1–4, 7
Ignatius (17 Oct): *also* Philippians 3.7–12; John 6.52–58
James Hannington (29 Oct): *especially* Matthew 10.28–39
Janani Luwum (17 Feb): *also* Ecclesiasticus 4.20–28; John 12.24–32
John Coleridge Patteson (20 Sept): *especially* 2 Chronicles 24.17–21; *also* Acts 7.55–end
Justin (1 June): *especially* John 15.18–21; *also* 1 Maccabees 2.15–22; 1 Corinthians 1.18–25
Laurence (10 Aug): *also* 2 Corinthians 9.6–10
Lucy (13 Dec): *also* Wisdom 3.1–7; 2 Corinthians 4.6–15
Oswald (5 Aug): *especially* 1 Peter 4.12–end; John 16.29–end
Perpetua, Felicity and comps (7 Mar): *especially* Revelation 12.10–12a; *also* Wisdom 3.1–7
Polycarp (23 Feb): *also* Revelation 2.8–11
Thomas Becket (29 Dec *or* 7 Jul): *especially* Matthew 10.28–33; *also* Ecclesiasticus 51.1–8
William Tyndale (6 Oct): *also* Proverbs 8.4–11; 2 Timothy 3.12–end

Teachers of the Faith and Spiritual Writers

I Kings 3.[6–10] 11–14; Proverbs 4.1–9; Wisdom 7.7–10, 15–16; Ecclesiasticus 39.1–10
Psalms 19.7–10; 34.11–17; 37.31–35; 119.89–96; 119.97–104
I Corinthians 1.18–25; *or* 2.1–10; *or* 2.9–end; Ephesians 3.8–12; 2 Timothy 4.1–8;
    Titus 2.1–8
Matthew 5.13–19; *or* 13.52–end; *or* 23.8–12; Mark 4.1–9; John 16.12–15

Ambrose (7 Dec): *also* Isaiah 41.9b–13; Luke 22.24–30
Anselm (21 Apr): *also* Wisdom 9.13–end; Romans 5.8–11
Athanasius (2 May): *also* Ecclesiasticus 4.20–28; *also* Matthew 10.24–27
Augustine of Hippo (28 Aug): *especially* Ecclesiasticus 39.1–10; *also* Romans 13.11–13
Basil and Gregory (2 Jan): *especially* 2 Timothy 4.1–8; Matthew 5.13–19
Bernard (20 Aug): *especially* Revelation 19.5–9
Catherine of Siena (29 Apr): *also* Proverbs 8.1, 6–11; John 17.12–end
Francis de Sales (24 Jan): *also* Proverbs 3.13–18; John 3.17–21
Gregory the Great (3 Sept): *also* I Thessalonians 2.3–8
Gregory of Nyssa and Macrina (19 July): *especially* I Corinthians 2.9–13;
    also Wisdom 9.13–17
Hilary (13 Jan): *also* I John 2.18–25; John 8.25–32
Irenaeus (28 June): *also* 2 Peter 1.16–end
Jeremy Taylor (13 Aug): *also* Titus 2.7–8, 11–14
John Bunyan (30 Aug): *also* Hebrews 12.1–2; Luke 21.21, 34–36
John Chrysostom (13 Sept): *especially* Matthew 5.13–19; *also* Jeremiah 1.4–10
John of the Cross (14 Dec): *especially* I Corinthians 2.1–10; *also* John 14.18–23
Leo (10 Nov): *also* I Peter 5.1–11
Richard Hooker (3 Nov): *especially* John 16.12–15; *also* Ecclesiasticus 44.10–15
Teresa of Avila (15 Oct): *also* Romans 8.22–27
Thomas Aquinas (28 Jan): *especially* Wisdom 7.7–10, 15–16; I Corinthians 2.9–end;
    John 16.12–15
William Law (10 Apr): *especially* I Corinthians 2.9–end; *also* Matthew 17.1–9

Bishops and Other Pastors

1 Samuel 16.1, 6–13; Isaiah 6.1–8; Jeremiah 1.4–10; Ezekiel 3.16–21; Malachi 2.5–7
Psalms 1; 15; 16.5–end; 96; 110
Acts 20.28–35; 1 Corinthians 4.1–5; 2 Corinthians 4.1–10 [or 1–2, 5–7];
    or 5.14–20; 1 Peter 5.1–4
Matthew 11.25–end; or 24.42–46; John 10.11–16; or 15.9–17; or 21.15–17

Augustine of Canterbury (26 May): also 1 Thessalonians 2.2b–8; Matthew 13.31–33
Charles Simeon (13 Nov): especially Malachi 2.5–7; also Colossians 1.3–8; Luke 8.4–8
David (1 Mar): also 2 Samuel 23.1–4; Psalm 89.19–22, 24
Dunstan (19 May): especially Matthew 24.42–46; also Exodus 31.1–5
Edward King (8 Mar): also Hebrews 13.1–8
George Herbert (27 Feb): especially Malachi 2.5–7; Matthew 11.25–end;
    also Revelation 19.5–9
Hugh (17 Nov): also 1 Timothy 6.11–16
John Keble (14 July): also Lamentations 3.19–26; Matthew 5.1–8
John and Charles Wesley (24 May): also Ephesians 5.15–20
Lancelot Andrewes (25 Sept): especially Isaiah 6.1–8
Martin of Tours (11 Nov): also 1 Thessalonians 5.1–11; Matthew 25.34–40
Nicholas (6 Dec): also Isaiah 61.1–3; 1 Timothy 6.6–11; Mark 10.13–16
Richard (16 June): also John 21.15–19
Swithun (15 July): also James 5.7–11, 13–18
Thomas Ken (8 June): especially 2 Corinthians 4.1–10 [or 1–2, 5–7]; Matthew 24.42–46
Wulfstan (19 Jan): especially Matthew 24.42–46

Members of Religious Communities

I Kings 19.9–18; Proverbs 10.27–end; Song of Solomon 8.6–7; Isaiah 61.10—62.5;
    Hosea 2.14–15, 19–20
Psalms 34.1–8; 112.1–9; 119.57–64; 123; 131
Acts 4.32–35; 2 Corinthians 10.17—11.2; Philippians 3.7–14; I John 2.15–17;
    Revelation 19.1, 5–9
Matthew 11.25–end; or 19.3–12; or 19.23–end; Luke 9.57–end; or 12.32–37

Aelred (12 Jan): also Ecclesiasticus 15.1–6
Alcuin (20 May): also Colossians 3.12–16; John 4.19–24
Antony (17 Jan): especially Philippians 3.7–14, also Matthew 19.16–26
Bede (25 May): also Ecclesiasticus 39.1–10
Benedict (11 July): also I Corinthians 3.10–11; Luke 18.18–22
Clare (11 Aug): especially Song of Solomon 8.6–7
Dominic (8 Aug): also Ecclesiasticus 39.1–10
Etheldreda (23 June): also Matthew 25.1–13
Francis of Assisi (4 Oct): also Galatians 6.14–end; Luke 12.22–34
Hilda (19 Nov): especially Isaiah 61.10—62.5
Hildegard (17 Sept): also I Corinthians 2.9–13; Luke 10.21–24
Julian of Norwich (8 May): also I Corinthians 13.8–end; Matthew 5.13–16
Vincent de Paul (27 Sept): also I Corinthians 1.25–end; Matthew 25.34–40

Missionaries

Isaiah 52.7–10; or 61.1–3a; Ezekiel 34.11–16; Jonah 3.1–5
Psalms 67; or 87; or 97; or 100; or 117
Acts 2.14, 22–36; or 13.46–49; or 16.6–10; or 26.19–23; Romans 15.17–21;
    2 Corinthians 5.11—6.2
Matthew 9.35–end; or 28.16–end; Mark 16.15–20; Luke 5.1–11; or 10.1–9

Aidan (31 Aug): also I Corinthians 9.16–19
Anskar (3 Feb): especially Isaiah 52.7–10; also Romans 10.11–15
Chad (2 Mar or 26 Oct): also I Timothy 6.11b–16
Columba (9 June): also Titus 2.11–end
Cuthbert (20 Mar or 4 Sept): especially Ezekiel 34.11–16; also Matthew 18.12–14
Cyril and Methodius (14 Feb): especially Isaiah 52.7–10; also Romans 10.11–15
Henry Martyn (19 Oct): especially Mark 16.15–end; also Isaiah 55.6–11
Ninian (16 Sept): especially Acts 13.46–49; Mark 16.15–end
Patrick (17 Mar): also Psalm 91.1–4, 13–16; Luke 10.1–12, 17–20
Paulinus (10 Oct): especially Matthew 28.16–end
Wilfrid (12 Oct): especially Luke 5.1–11; also I Corinthians 1.18–25
Willibrord (7 Nov): especially Isaiah 52.7–10; Matthew 28.16–end

Any Saint

General

Genesis 12.1–4; Proverbs 8.1–11; Micah 6.6–8; Ecclesiasticus 2.7–13 [14–end]
Psalms 32; 33.1–5; 119.1–8; 139.1–4 [5–12]; 145.8–14
Ephesians 3.14–19; or 6.11–18; Hebrews 13.7–8, 15–16; James 2.14–17;
        1 John 4.7–16; Revelation 21.[1–4] 5–7
Matthew 19.16–21; or 25.1–13; or 25.14–30; John 15.1–8; or 17.20–end

Christian rulers

1 Samuel 16.1–13a; 1 Kings 3.3–14
Psalms 72.1–7; 99
1 Timothy 2.1–6
Mark 10.42–45; Luke 14.27–33

Alfred the Great (26 Oct): also 2 Samuel 23.1–5; John 18.33–37
Edward the Confessor (13 Oct): also 2 Samuel 23.1–5; 1 John 4.13–16
Margaret of Scotland (16 Nov): also Proverbs 31.10–12, 20, 26–end;
        1 Corinthians 12.13—13.3; Matthew 25.34–end

Those working for the poor and underprivileged

Isaiah 58.6–11
Psalms 82; 146.5–10
Hebrews 13.1–3; 1 John 3.14–18
Matthew 5.1–12; or 25.31–end

Elizabeth of Hungary (18 Nov): especially Matthew 25.31–end; also Proverbs 31.10–end
Josephine Butler (30 May): especially Isaiah 58.6–11; also 1 John 3.18–23; Matthew 9.10–13
William Wilberforce, Olaudah Equiano and Thomas Clarkson (30 July): also Job 31.16–23;
Galatians 3.26–end, 4.6–7; Luke 4.16–21

Men and women of learning

Proverbs 8.22–31; Ecclesiasticus 44.1–15
Psalms 36.5–10; 49.1–4
Philippians 4.7–8
Matthew 13.44–46, 52; John 7.14–18

Those whose holiness was revealed in marriage and family life

Proverbs 31.10–13, 19–20, 30–end; Tobit 8.4–7
Psalms 127; 128
1 Peter 3.1–9
Mark 3.31–end; Luke 10.38–end

Mary Sumner (9 Aug): also Hebrews 13.1–5
Monica (27 Aug): also Ecclesiasticus 26.1–3, 13–16

The Guidance of the Holy Spirit

Proverbs 24.3–7; Isaiah 30.15–21; Wisdom 9.13–17
Psalms 25.1–9; 104.26–33; 143.8–10
Acts 15.23–29; Romans 8:22–27; 1 Corinthians 12.4–13
Luke 14.27–33; John 14.23–26; *or* 16.13–15

Rogation Days
(6–8 May in 2013)

Deuteronomy 8.1–10; 1 Kings 8.35–40; Job 28.1–11
Psalms 104.21–30; 107.1–9; 121
Philippians 4.4–7; 2 Thessalonians 3.6–13; 1 John 5.12–15
Matthew 6.1–15; Mark 11.22–24; Luke 11.5–13

Harvest Thanksgiving

Year A	Year B	Year C
Deuteronomy 8.7–18 *or* 28.1–14	Joel 2.21–27	Deuteronomy 26.1–11
Psalm 65	Psalm 126	Psalm 100
2 Corinthians 9.6–end	1 Timothy 2.1–7 *or* 6.6–10	Philippians 4.4–9
Luke 12.16–30 *or* 17.11–19	Matthew 6.25–33	*or* Revelation 14.14–18
		John 6.25–35

Mission and Evangelism

Isaiah 49.1–6; *or* 52.7–10; Micah 4.1–5
Psalms 2; 46; 67
Acts 17.10–end; 2 Corinthians 5.14—6.2; Ephesians 2.13–end
Matthew 5.13–16; *or* 28.16–end; John 17.20–end

The Unity of the Church

Jeremiah 33.6–9*a*; Ezekiel 36.23–28; Zephaniah 3.16–end
Psalms 100; 122; 133
Ephesians 4.1–6; Colossians 3.9–17; 1 John 4.9–15
Matthew 18.19–22; John 11.45–52; *or* 17.11*b*–23

The Peace of the World

Isaiah 9.1–6; *or* 57.15–19; Micah 4.1–5
Psalms 40.14–17; 72.1–7; 85.8–13
Philippians 4.6–9; 1 Timothy 2.1–6; James 3.13–18
Matthew 5.43–end; John 14.23–29; *or* 15.9–17

Social Justice and Responsibility

Isaiah 32.15–end; Amos 5.21–24; or 8.4–7; Acts 5.1–11
Psalms 31.21–24; 85.1–7; 146.5–10
Colossians 3.12–15; James 2.1–4
Matthew 5.1–12; or 25.31–end; Luke 16.19–end

Ministry, including Ember Days
(See page 7)

Numbers 11.16–17, 24–29; or 27.15–end; 1 Samuel 16.1–13a; Isaiah 6.1–8;
    or 61.1–3; Jeremiah 1.4–10
Psalms 40.8–13; 84.8–12; 89.19–25; 101.1–5, 7; 122
Acts 20.28–35; 1 Corinthians 3.3–11; Ephesians 4.4–16; Philippians 3.7–14
Luke 4.16–21; or 12.35–43; or 22.24–27; John 4.31–38; or 15.5–17

In Time of Trouble

Genesis 9.8–17; Job 1.13–end; Isaiah 38.6–11
Psalms 86.1–7; 107.4–15; 142.1–7
Romans 3.21–26; Romans 8.18–25; 2 Corinthians 8.1–5, 9
Mark 4.35–end; Luke 12.1–7; John 16.31–end

For the Sovereign

Joshua 1.1–9; Proverbs 8.1–16
Psalms 20; 101; 121
Romans 13.1–10; Revelation 21.22—22.4
Matthew 22.16–22; Luke 22.24–30

The anniversary of HM The Queen's accession is 6 February.

Psalms in the Course of a Month

*The following provision may be used for a monthly cycle of psalmody in place of the psalms
provided in the tables in this booklet. It is based on the provision in* The Book of Common Prayer.

	Morning Prayer	Evening Prayer
1	1—5	6—8
2	9—11	12—14
3	15—17	18
4	19—21	22—23
5	24—26	27—29
6	30—31	32—34
7	35—36	37
8	38—40	41—43
9	44—46	47—49
10	50—52	53—55
11	56—58	59—61
12	62—64	65—67
13	68	69—70
14	71—72	73—74
15	75—77	78
16	79—81	82—85
17	86—88	89
18	90—92	93—94
19	95—97	98—101
20	102—103	104
21	105	106
22	107	108—109
23	110—112	113—115
24	116—118	119.1–32
25	119.33–72	119.73–96
26	119.97–144	119.145–176
27	120—125	126—131
28	132—135	136—138
29	139—140	141—143
30	144—146	147—150

In February the psalms are read only to the 28th or 29th day of the month.

In January, March, May, July, August, October and December, all of which have 31 days,
the same psalms are read on the last day of the month (being an ordinary weekday) which
were read the day before, or else the psalms of the monthly course omitted on one of the
Sundays in that month.

Concise Calendar November 2013 – December 2014

Advent 2013 to the eve of Advent 2014: Year A (Daily Eucharistic Lectionary Year 2)

November 2013					
Sunday		4bAdv	3bAdv	2bAdv	ChrK
Monday		4	11	18	25
Tuesday		5	12	19	26
Wednesday		6	13	20	27
Thursday		7	14	21	28
Friday	AllSS	8	15	22	29
Saturday	2	9	16	23	30

December 2013					
Sunday	Adv1	Adv2	Adv3	Adv4	Chr1
Monday	2	9	16	23	30
Tuesday	3	10	17	24	31
Wednesday	4	11	18	Chr	
Thursday	5	12	19	26	
Friday	6	13	20	27	
Saturday	7	14	21	28	

January 2014					
Sunday		Chr2	Bapt	Ep2	Ep3
Monday		Epiph	13	20	27
Tuesday		7	14	21	28
Wednesday	1	8	15	22	29
Thursday	2	9	16	23	30
Friday	3	10	17	24	31
Saturday	4	11	18	25	

February 2014					
Sunday		Pres	4bLnt	3bLnt	2bLnt
Monday		3	10	17	24
Tuesday		4	11	18	25
Wednesday		5	12	19	26
Thursday		6	13	20	27
Friday		7	14	21	28
Saturday	1	8	15	22	

March 2014						
Sunday		SbLnt	Lnt1	Lnt2	Lnt3	Lnt4
Monday		3	10	17	24	31
Tuesday		4	11	18	Ann	
Wednesday		AshW	12	19	26	
Thursday		6	13	20	27	
Friday		7	14	21	28	
Saturday	1	8	15	22	29	

April 2014					
Sunday		Lnt5	PmS	Est	Est2
Monday		7	14	21	28
Tuesday	1	8	15	22	29
Wednesday	2	9	16	23	30
Thursday	3	10	MTh	24	
Friday	4	11	GFr	25	
Saturday	5	12	19	26	

May 2014					
Sunday		Est3	Est4	Est5	Est6
Monday		5	12	19	26
Tuesday		6	13	20	27
Wednesday		7	14	21	28
Thursday	1	8	15	22	Ascn
Friday	2	9	16	23	30
Saturday	3	10	17	24	31

June 2014					
Sunday	Est7	Pent	TrS	Tr1	Tr2
Monday	2	9	16	23	30
Tuesday	3	10	17	24	
Wednesday	4	11	18	25	
Thursday	5	12	19	26	
Friday	6	13	20	27	
Saturday	7	14	21	28	

July 2014					
Sunday		Tr3	Tr4	Tr5	Tr6
Monday		7	14	21	28
Tuesday	1	8	15	22	29
Wednesday	2	9	16	23	30
Thursday	3	10	17	24	31
Friday	4	11	18	25	
Saturday	5	12	19	26	

August 2014						
Sunday		Tr7	Tr8	Tr9	Tr10	Tr11
Monday		4	11	18	25	
Tuesday		5	12	19	26	
Wednesday		6	13	20	27	
Thursday		7	14	21	28	
Friday	1	8	15	22	29	
Saturday	2	9	16	23	30	

September 2014					
Sunday		Tr12	Tr13	Tr14	Tr15
Monday	1	8	15	22	29
Tuesday	2	9	16	23	30
Wednesday	3	10	17	24	
Thursday	4	11	18	25	
Friday	5	12	19	26	
Saturday	6	13	20	27	

October 2014					
Sunday		Tr16	Tr17	Tr18	LstTr
Monday		6	13	20	27
Tuesday		7	14	21	28
Wednesday	1	8	15	22	29
Thursday	2	9	16	23	30
Friday	3	10	17	24	31
Saturday	4	11	18	25	

November 2014						
Sunday		4bAdv	3bAdv	2bAdv	ChrK	Adv1
Monday		3	10	17	24	
Tuesday		4	11	18	25	
Wednesday		5	12	19	26	
Thursday		6	13	20	27	
Friday		7	14	21	28	
Saturday	AllSS	8	15	22	29	

December 2014					
Sunday		Adv2	Adv3	Adv4	Chr1
Monday	1	8	15	22	29
Tuesday	2	9	16	23	30
Wednesday	3	10	17	24	31
Thursday	4	11	18	Chr	
Friday	5	12	19	26	
Saturday	6	13	20	27	

On Sunday 5 January The Epiphany may be celebrated, transferred from 6 January.

On Sunday 29 June Peter and Paul, Apostles may be celebrated.

On Sunday 24 August Bartholomew the Apostle may be celebrated.

On Sunday 14 September Holy Cross Day may be celebrated.

On Sunday 21 September Matthew, Apostle and Evangelist may be celebrated.

On Sunday 2 November All Saints' Day may be celebrated, transferred from 1 November.

On Sunday 28 December The Holy Innocents may be celebrated.